THE ORVIS

— GUIDE TO —

BEGINNING SALTWATER FLY FISHING

THE ORVIS®
— GUIDE TO —
BEGINNING SALTWATER FLY FISHING

101 TIPS for the **absolute beginner**

Conway X. Bowman

Foreword by Kirk Deeter

Illustrations by Bob White

Skyhorse Publishing

Skyhorse Publishing books may be purchased in bulk at special discounts for sales promotion, corporate gifts, fund-raising, or educational purposes. Special editions can also be created to specifications. For details, contact the Special Sales Department, Skyhorse Publishing, 307 West 36th Street, 11th Floor, New York, NY 10018 or info@skyhorsepublishing.com.

www.skyhorsepublishing.com

10 9 8 7 6 5 4 3 2

Library of Congress Cataloging-in-Publication Data

Bowman, Conway X.
  The Orvis guide to beginning saltwater fly fishing : 101 tips for the absolute beginner / by Conway X. Bowman.
      p. cm.
  ISBN 978-1-61608-090-7 (pbk. : alk. paper)
  1. Fly fishing. I. Orvis Company. II. Title.
  SH456.B675 2010
  799.16--dc22
                                      2010034981
Printed in China

This book is dedicated to my father, John Bowman, to whom I'm grateful for taking the time to take me fishing and lighting the fire that fuels my passion for fly fishing and the natural world today. His gentle guidance and firm conviction have molded me into the husband, father, and man I am today. I love you, Pop.

Contents

Foreword

WHEN YOU PLAY WITH SHARKS FOR FUN—USING FLY tackle, no less—people are bound to assume you're a little twisted.

That's certainly what I expected of Conway Bowman, the world's best-known "fly fishing for mako sharks guy," when I set out to write a story about his exploits for *Field & Stream* magazine several years ago. (The story, by the way, culminated with Conway fighting a 150-pound mako, twenty miles off La Jolla . . . from a kayak).

I've since learned, however, that the man known best for operating on the angling world's ragged edge is also one of the most grounded, meticulous, and passionate fly fishers around. Conway would be just as enthralled with the challenge of presenting tiny flies to sardines as he would be casting bunny flies at laid-up tarpon, or teasing mako sharks to bite on fleshy flies. Well almost, anyway.

Conway is a problem solver, which is essential to being an effective fly angler, especially in the salt. Of all the anglers I've fished with in salty places, Bowman is the best, bar none. He's in a league of his own. He has respected his elders, and embraced the traditions of this sport. By the same token, he's pushed boundaries far beyond where others (old and young) are willing to dabble.

When fishing with Bowman, one gets the sense that his acumen has less to do with the beautiful loops he tosses from a nine-foot rod and more to do with the intangibles. All of that starts with passion.

Conway's passion is rooted in fly fishing for sharks. He first got into the sport to satisfy an itch to tangle with the biggest, fastest aquatic creatures a young guy from San Diego with a fly rod might encounter. He spent hours and hours on the sharking grounds, learning about the fish, their habits, their moods, what they would take, and why. In time, Bowman molded himself into a superlative fly fisherman.

His passion has taken him fishing all over the world, from the Louisiana marshes to Belize, Florida, the Baja Peninsula, and other salty places that many anglers can only dream about. Along the way, he has caught all sorts of species, including the world record for redfish caught on the fly.

In this book, Conway has taken all he has learned on the water and presented it in a straightforward manner. He's done this without focusing so much on the "what" or the "where," but rather on the "how" and "why." Lefty Kreh once said that the mission of a great guide isn't to demonstrate his knowledge; rather, it's to *share* it in a way that other people can grab onto and understand, then use themselves. In *The ORVIS Guide to Beginning Saltwater Fly Fishing*, Conway has done just that.

Reading through the pages of this book, I felt as if I were right there with Conway, in a flats skiff, or wading in skinny water . . . and I could hear him talking. I'm lucky to count such experiences among my favorite real-life saltwater memories. And I'll gratefully take these book lessons with me (new wrinkles included) wherever I fish.

The highest praise one writer can give to another is to say he hears the voice, feels the essence, and learns from the experience of reading the words on written pages. That's what I'm saying here. Conway has poured it all out . . . gracefully, eloquently, and honestly. I am grateful that he has done so. And I am sure you will feel the same way.

—**Kirk Deeter**
Editor-at-Large, *Field & Stream*
Coauthor, *The Little Red Book of Fly Fishing*

Introduction

WHEN TOM ROSENBAUER AT ORVIS ASKED ME TO write *The ORVIS Guide to Beginning Saltwater Fly Fishing,* I was honored. An opportunity like this does not present itself very often—so I accepted with excitement and some anxiety. I went for it! I have never considered myself a writer. Yes, I've written articles for various fly-fishing magazines over the past fifteen years or so, but to write a book on the how-tos in fly fishing seemed daunting at first. I've been guiding fly fishers for the better part of thirty years, cutting my teeth as a kid taking family members, friends, and anyone else who wanted to fish on the many creeks and rivers in Idaho's Sawtooth Mountains. After that, I logged many years on my home waters off the San Diego coast, searching for tuna, yellowtail, and mako sharks from the deck of my sixteen-foot skiff. It was on these deep Pacific trips that I realized I had a talent for grasping and understanding the ocean environment and the fish that lived there. From fishing with other people, I also realized that I had the ability to communicate the basics of fly fishing.

This book follows in the giant footsteps of the true pioneers of this wonderful sport. And no one has left a bigger footprint than has Lefty Kreh. I believe that much of what we know today about saltwater fly fishing comes from the pages of Lefty's many books, and from his dedication and unselfish sharing of his knowledge with all fly fishers, veteran and novice alike.

I place much of the blame for my "addiction" to saltwater fly fishing on a friend and mentor, Nick Curcione, another saltwater fly-fishing icon, who kindled my interest in the pursuit of the shortfin mako sharks close to my home in San Diego. Nick, like Lefty, has authored many books on the subject over the years, but none as important to me as *The ORVIS Guide to Saltwater Fly*

Fishing. That book led to my becoming a saltwater fly fisherman and one of the most vocal proponents of the sport. It didn't take me long to realize the fly-fishing potential that lay but a double haul from my back porch. Nick's progressive casting techniques with shooting heads, and his mastery of fighting big fish on the fly, have had a big influence on me.

I can remember as a youngster (eight or nine years old) sitting on the floor of my father's study, thumbing through books by Lefty, Nick, and Stu Apte, my eyes riveted on pictures of giant tarpon, snook, and sharks that these master anglers had caught on flies. I was fascinated by the environments they were fishing, tropical places like Belize, Florida, and Costa Rica, destinations that offered anglers the opportunity to fish waters that were a far cry from the trout streams most fly fishers were used to. That's what attracted me: This was fly fishing on the ragged edge! Even way back then, I knew that I wanted to catch big fish on the fly rod in exotic locales.

My conversion into a saltwater fly fisherman did not happen overnight—it was a slow process. I was born and raised in San Diego, California, a city long known for its temperate climate, as well as its proximity to Tijuana, Mexico. For anglers, it offered access to some of the best saltwater fishing in the United States. My buddies and I spin-fished or fished from half-day boats in the kelp beds for bonito, yellowtail, and barracudas, or hit local lakes and ponds for largemouths, crappies, and bluegills. A few locals fly-fished for these freshwater species—only one man, Sam Nix, used a fly rod for fishing salt water. Nix, an older man who had fly-fished San Diego's bays and jetties since the 1930s, was a legend to some folks, but to many fishermen he was an eccentric. One thing is a matter of record: He caught saltwater fish with a fly rod, a practice that was practically unheard of back then. In 1977, however, something happened that helped me see the light.

That summer, my father was hired to work as a fishing guide at a lodge in Idaho's Sawtooth Valley. Each summer for four years, Dad and I would spend two months living in a house trailer on the shores of Redfish Lake, just a short drive from classic trout streams in Idaho, Montana, and Wyoming. With an inexpensive fly rod and reel, I caught my first fly rod fish, a rainbow trout, out of the spring-fed waters of Silver Creek, only a few miles from Sun Valley. I was six and, like the 'bow, I was hooked. Enter Bill and Eileen Stroud.

Bill and Eileen Stroud, my surrogate uncle and aunt, owned and operated the only real fly shop in San Diego. When not fishing or duck hunting, my father and I would hang out there, rummaging through trays of flies or just talking fly fishing with this wonderful couple. They were the ones who first took me out on a "cattle boat," where they taught me the finer points of saltwater angling. More important, they introduced me to the world of saltwater fly fishing.

Years later, as a young man, I began walking the local beaches, fly rod in hand, casting flies to corbina and surf perch feeding along the surf line. Then, in my early twenties, I bought a sixteen-foot aluminum boat with a tiller-controlled twenty-five-horsepower motor and began venturing offshore in search of sharks, bonito, and yellowtail. Those early journeys helped me learn about the ocean, and eventually led me to a career as a fly-fishing guide.

No matter where you are, be it a distant tropical location or a beach or estuary close to home, or what you're fishing for, from snapper to bluefish to gigantic blue marlin, you'll find that fly fishing saltwater is an exciting, challenging, and rewarding sport. It's my hope that this book will help you along your journey.

Great tides . . .

—Conway X. Bowman

PART

1

Getting Started

1

Learn from the conventional fishermen

YOU CAN LEARN A LOT ABOUT CATCHING FISH ON the fly from the conventional spinning and casting rod anglers. The spin-and-cast guys are just as hardcore and passionate about saltwater fishing as fly fishers. These folks can teach you something about what types of flies to select, how to fight fish, how to read the water, the best knots to tie, and what to look for when you're fishing. If you don't come off as an elitist, as some fly fishermen do, one of these guys may even invite you to go out on his boat for a day of striper fishing, or to go check out one of his favorite surf-fishing spots. Pay attention, because you'll learn things that you will never find in a book. Remember the adage that "Experience is the best teacher."

Many of the most skilled and knowledgeable saltwater fly fishermen are also outstanding spin-and-cast anglers, people who have honed their skills by casting with a surf rod and/or jig fishing from a boat. Learning to cast a spinning outfit well will also make you a better fly caster. Why? Because being able to cast a small jig accurately into a small space, like a mangrove or along a shoreline, will help you refine your fly-casting abilities.

Another example of learning from a conventional guy: The "old salt" you routinely find hanging around the local dock or tackle shop is a wealth of information, even if he has never held a fly rod. There's a good chance that he has logs of his countless hours spent fishing the salt, and has probably caught more than his share of saltwater gamefish. Many of these guys love to talk about fishing in the "good ol' days." Get them started and stand by—they will regale you with tales about the old days that are not only interesting, but also educational.

The beginning fly fisherman can learn a lot from a guy like my father, who's been fishing most of his life.

2

Fish with a buddy, find a mentor, go to a trade show

FISHING WITH A FRIEND IS ONE OF THE GREATEST joys of being out on the water. You can share the experiences of catching your first redfish, hooking the first bonito of the season, or finding that flat or beach that has never felt wading shoes. Often, it's not even about the fish or fishing, but about appreciating the surroundings and sharing a few laughs. Perhaps you can share knowledge about knots and flies, or critique each other's casting skills. If so inclined, the two of you can join a local fly-fishing club or fly-tying class, where you can absorb and share all sorts of information with other saltwater fly enthusiasts.

If you are a newcomer to saltwater fly fishing, find a mentor who will take you under his wing and teach you everything that's important to becoming a proficient saltwater fly angler. There's a given about fly fishers, no matter if they prefer salt or fresh water: They are not loners. They love fellow fly anglers, especially those folks just entering the sport, and will gladly jaw with you for hours about fishing, sharing their experiences. Where does one find a mentor? Visit your local fly shop or join a fly-fishing club.

Another great source for learning is the fishing trade show. In fact, trade shows are where I began gathering information about fly fishing the salt. A Southern Californian by birth, I had the chance to speak with the pioneers of saltwater fly fishing only at the West

Good friend. Good fishing. Great times!

Coast fishing trade shows. It was at these shows that I had the chance to speak with my childhood saltwater fly-fishing heroes such as Lefty Kreh, Nick Curcione, Flip Pallot, and Dan Blanton. Every year, I looked forward to these shows and the opportunity to speak with and learn from these outstanding anglers.

PART

2

Equipment

3

How to choose a
basic saltwater outfit

GETTING STARTED IN SALTWATER FLY FISHING CAN
seem like an overwhelming task, but it isn't complicated. It's most
important to buy the right rod and reel for the type of fishing you'll
be doing. The East Coast striper fly fisherman will require a very
different outfit from what a West Coast surf perch fisherman needs,
and the guy interested in catching redfish in the Louisiana marsh
will need a vastly different rig from the angler casting to bonito off
a jetty in Southern California. Here are my suggestions:

The Rod

Choose a seven- or eight-weight rod. This is the perfect starter
rod for the beginning saltwater fly fisher, heavy enough to punch a
fly into a stiff wind, yet light enough to cast all day. Technically, you
could use a heavy trout rod, but ideally you want to use a saltwater
rod because it's made of materials that can handle salt, sand, and
generally tough conditions.

The Reel

A good direct-drive reel that can hold a minimum of 200 yards
of thirty-pound Dacron backing will work well in most saltwater
fly-fishing situations. Currently, fly reels designed for saltwater fishing are more than adequate in handling fish up to fifty pounds. Buy
an extra spool to hold your shooting head.

Fly Lines

Here is what you'll need:

1. A basic weight-forward (WF) floating line matched to the weight of your fly rod. The WF floating line is a great all-around fly line for sight-casting in shallow water. Don't get confused by all the marketing of "saltwater tapers," "bonefish tapers," or "redfish tapers." Such lines are for more advanced, specialized fly fishers, not beginners.

2. A weighted shooting head. A combination of a weighted front taper and an intermediate running line, this is ideal for sub-surface fishing or fishing rip currents from the beach. When fish are feeding below the surface, the shooting head will keep your fly in the hit zone longer. A 250- to 300-grain should be sufficient for most situations. The grain weight equals the sink rate of the fly line, so a 250- to 300-grain line will sink between five and eight inches per second. This is plenty of sink rate to get you down to feeding fish.

A basic rod matched with a quality reel is a
good starting point for a beginner.

4

Saltwater
fly rod length

THE STANDARD NINE-FOOT FLY ROD WORKS BEST IN many saltwater fly-fishing situations. It provides the angler with enough length to keep his fly line high off the water while back-casting and is effective when fighting fish in shallow water.

Many beach fly fishermen prefer a longer fly rod, something in the ten- or eleven-foot range. The added length assists in keeping the fly line safely above the shoreline structure on the backcast. This also allows for the shooting and/or weight-forward section of the fly line to extend beyond the rod's tip section, providing much-needed assistance in shooting the fly line as well as extending the length of the cast.

For bluewater fly fishing, a shorter rod (eight to eight and a half feet) works best when fighting a fish in deep water. A stiff butt section is especially important for putting pressure on a fish when reeling it in from deep water. It also saves the angler a trip to his chiropractor for an adjustment on his sacrum.

A shorter rod is best when you're fishing for bluewater fish such as tuna, sharks, and billfish.

5

What makes a good saltwater fly reel?

A GOOD SALTWATER FLY REEL SHOULD BE MADE from first-grade aluminum bar stock, have a slightly oversized handle that can be easily cranked while fighting a fish, and, most important, have a strong drag system.

The drag system is the heart of a good saltwater reel—it is essential in controlling the powerful surge of a gamefish that's determined to escape. A disk drag system of cork, Rulon, or graphite will stand up to the long, strong fights of saltwater gamefish. Many of the stacked-disk-drag fly reels on today's market are outstanding and require little special maintenance. The cork-drag reel has the most powerful drag system; however, such reels require a bit of TLC. Oiling and lubricating the cork drag are essential to retaining its excellent action.

For both synthetic and cork fly reels, back off the drag at the end of each fishing day or if the reel is not to be used for a long time. This will help preserve the drag and keep it working in top form on future trips.

A quality saltwater fly reel is a smart investment. ▶

6

Drag setting for saltwater fly fishing

PROPER DRAG SETTINGS ARE ESSENTIAL FOR SALT-water fly fishing. A proper setting can spell the difference between landing and losing the fish of a lifetime. Unlike conventional or spinning reels—on which the drag is usually preset and not adjusted during the fight—the fly reel drag can be manipulated by applying pressure to the reel with palm or fingers, giving the angler more control over the amount of pressure needed throughout the fight.

To set the drag, take your fly reel and tighten the drag so there is only light tension on the reel as you pull off line with your free hand; then tighten the drag until you feel resistance.

Begin fishing using a light drag. Once you have a fish on and the fight has begun, apply needed pressure by palming your reel—however, apply the pressure carefully so you don't break the tippet. Don't be surprised if you lose a few fish as you learn this method. It takes time and practice. Eventually, though, knowing when and how to apply pressure will become instinctive.

Palming the reel gives the angler more control ▶ when fighting a fish.

7

Using intermediate lines

INTERMEDIATE LINES DON'T FLOAT AND THEY DON'T sink rapidly. When you cast them out onto the water, they will sink very slowly, which makes them perfect choices when casting to fish feeding just below the surface (one to five feet) or in slightly deeper channels. You can use these versatile lines in situations as varied as casting to bonefish feeding off a reef in a channel or to West Coast yellowtail feeding just below the surface in the middle of the ocean.

When choosing your rod and corresponding fly line, base your choice on the type of fishing you intend to do, as a heavier intermediate line, such as an eight, will sink faster than a lighter line, such as a five.

In addition to getting the fly in the hit zone, the slick coating on an intermediate line will let you put extra length in your cast.

An intermediate fly line is perfect for fishing along reef channels. ▶

8

Using a sinking line

THE BEST SALTWATER FLY FISHING USUALLY TAKES place below the surface, whether you're fishing near shore or off-shore. Fish such as tuna, dorado, bluefish, and stripers will often feed in deep water, requiring anglers to get their flies deeper into the

Once mastered, the integrated shooting/sinking head is a joy to cast.

water column. This requires the use of a full-sinking line or sinking shooting head.

Full-Sinking Line

Full-sinking lines are rated Types I through V, I being the lightest and V the heaviest. If you are casting to fish only a few feet below the surface, a Type I or II shooting head will work fine. However, if the fish are feeding twenty feet down, the Type V would be your line of choice. The entire fly line is weighted, and is approximately one hundred feet long.

Integrated Sinking Shooting Head

These are my favorite sinking fly lines. The first twenty-six feet of these lines are weighted, and the rest is monocore running line. Due to the slick surface of the monocore running line, these fly lines cast like a dream. Additionally, since all the weight is loaded at the front end of the line, the momentum of the weighted section helps extend the distance of your cast. These lines are rated in grains, from 150 to 800 grains—150 is the lightest, 800 the heaviest. An 800-grain line will work most effectively to fish to thirty feet.

Lead-core Line

In depths over twenty-five feet, lead-core lines are usually the best choices. Because they sink so quickly, they work well when you're fishing from a drifting boat and when you're dealing with strong currents. They are typically twenty feet long, and are attached with a loop-to-loop connection to a monofilament running line. The weight of the lead-core line and the thin diameter of the mono running line allow these lines to get down faster when compared to the other types of sinking fly lines. However, they can be difficult to cast—not only that, but the mono running line has a tendency to coil while casting.

9

Does fly line color matter in salt water?

TODAY'S FLY FISHERMAN CAN BUY FLY LINES IN A wide variety of colors. Before settling on a color, consider its advantages and disadvantages. If you buy a brightly colored line, for example, you'll be able to follow a hooked fish's position in a fight. On the downside, many fish, especially those found in shallow, clear water, are skittish and easily spooked by brightly colored line.

Fly lines in natural colors (light blue, tan, or light green) are wise choices in most situations. Such colors make it easier to match the line color to the surroundings in which you plan to fish. On overcast, low-light days, gray and green lines are good choices; clear, sunny, blue-sky days seem best served by light blue lines; in rocky areas or light brown sandy waters, tan should be considered. Remember that one color does not suit all conditions.

Fly lines in light blue, tan, or light green are good choices for salt water.

10

Backing: weight and quantity demands

LOSING A BIG SALTWATER GAMEFISH AFTER IT IS hooked and decides to head for the horizon is, in many instances, the result of filling your reel with backing that is either too short or too light.

Twenty-pound backing is a good choice for most inshore saltwater fly-fishing situations, while thirty-pound backing is better suited for larger bluewater gamefish.

Since many inshore saltwater gamefish will make initial runs of seventy-five to one hundred yards before they turn and settle into fighting mode, your fly reel should hold a minimum of 175 yards of twenty-pound Dacron backing.

For bluewater fly fishing, a minimum of 300 yards of thirty-pound Dacron or gel-spun polyethylene is standard. Big bluewater gamefish such as tuna and marlin will run off 200 yards of backing before you have time to say, "Come back and fight like a man!" These fish can also dive to great depths, thus making essential an abundant supply of backing.

Twenty- and thirty-pound Dacron backing are good choices for a saltwater fly reel. ▶

11

Best color for backing?

THE PHRASE "GETTING INTO YOUR BACKING" arouses excitement through a saltwater fly fisherman's being each time he hears it. There is nothing more exciting than witnessing one hundred yards of backing slicing through the water, pulled by a bonefish, tarpon, sailfish, or marlin. When this happens, the color of your backing is essential for tracking the fish's direction: Is it swimming at an angle, or is it sounding? Sooner or later, every saltwater fisherman is going to experience this.

High-visibility backing will help you determine how to fight a fish. For instance, when tarpon fishing it is important that you are able to turn a fish's head during the fight, a move aimed at keeping the tarpon off balance and assuring that it is brought quickly to the boat. Just as important, high-visibility backing allows the angler to track the fish's direction and keep applying pressure in the direction opposite from where it wants to go.

The best colors? I prefer bright yellow or bright orange, both highly visible backings regardless of weather conditions or water color.

Bright colors allow you to see where your fish is ▶ going during the fight.

12

Tying the backing to the fly reel

MANY FLY FISHERS DON'T KNOW HOW TO TIE THE backing to their fly reels. And why should they? Isn't backing usually wound onto your fly reel at the time of purchase? We have come to expect this courtesy from fly shops after buying a reel. However, if you ever need to change your fly line and attach new backing to your reel and find yourself miles from the nearest fly shop, being able to do it yourself will not only save you a lengthy trip to town but will also afford you more fishing time.

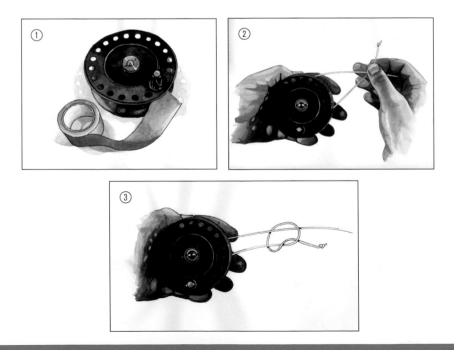

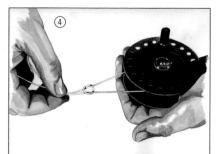

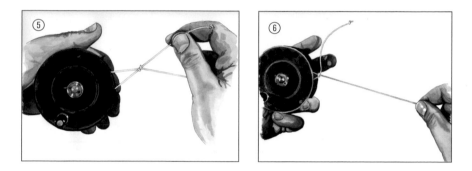

Gel-spun and Dacron backing have a tendency to slip once they are connected to the fly reel's arbor. A good way to avoid this problem is to wrap a strip of blue medical or gaffer's tape around the arbor before putting on the backing. The tape's surface will create just enough friction to prevent the backing from slipping as you wind it onto the reel.

The Arbor Knot is a good knot for tying backing to your fly reel's arbor. It is simple to tie and very low profile.

13

How to build a basic saltwater leader

THE LEADER IS THE MOST IMPORTANT CONNECTION between the saltwater fly fisherman and the fish. Tied incorrectly, it will place the angler at a distinct disadvantage in casting, especially under windy conditions.

Simple in its design, the saltwater fly leader can meet the demands of almost every saltwater fly-fishing situation. A leader's length varies depending on conditions, but a nine-foot leader will work in most situations; a "four-three-two combo" works well, as it allows the fly to roll over as it is cast. Creating this leader is fairly simple:

To start, tie a two-turn Surgeon's Loop of forty- or fifty-pound soft monofilament at the fly line's end; then join the sections of your leader with Blood Knots, applying saliva to the knots to guarantee a solid connection impervious to separation, taking care to test the strength of each knot as you complete it.

*four feet of forty-pound soft mono
*three feet of thirty-pound mono
*two feet of twenty-pound mono

Two-turn surgeon's loop.   Blood knot.

14

Choosing the best material for a wire leader

WHEN YOU FLY-FISH IN SALT WATER, THERE WILL BE times when you will be dealing with a toothy critter such as a barracuda, shark, needlefish, or Sierra mackerel—fish with sharp teeth

Single-strand stainless-steel wire is the best choice when targeting toothy critters such as mako sharks.

capable of severing the heaviest monofilament and fluorocarbon leaders. It is the savvy saltwater fly fisherman who has learned to attach a biteproof tippet to his fly line.

There are two schools of thought regarding biteproof tippet: One school favors a soft, stainless steel leader when fishing for toothed gamefish; the other prefers a single-strand stainless wire leader. Let's compare the two.

The soft stainless steel leader is easier to tie, but not as durable as the single-strand stainless wire leader. In a lengthy battle, chances are that a sharp-toothed fish is eventually going to bite through the soft stainless steel leader and break off.

The second option, and my personal preference, is the single-strand stainless wire leader. The wire is tough, able to withstand the raking teeth of a shark far better than soft a stainless steel leader. Another advantage of this type of leader is its small diameter. Like a piece of dental floss, it fits nicely between the fish's teeth and doesn't get worn, frayed, or chewed as the battle rages on.

If you decide to use a single-strand wire leader, the most common way of attaching it to your line is with a Haywire Twist. Although there are tools to assist you in tying this knot, I recommend the old-school method demonstrated in many fishing knot books.

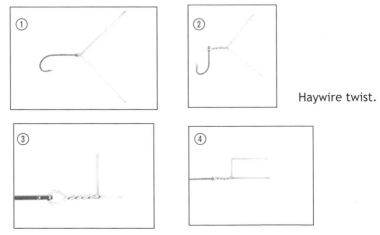

Haywire twist.

15

How long should a leader be for a sinking line?

BECAUSE WEIGHTED SHOOTING LINES AND SHOOTing heads sink, the leader need not be the standard nine feet. In fact, the shorter the leader, the faster the fly will sink into the fish's hit zone. Conversely, if the leader is too long, the fly will not keep pace with the line as it sinks, causing the leader and fly to end up higher in the water than the sinking line—a situation bound to create problems when gamefish are feeding at a certain depth.

Depending on how leader-shy the fish are, and to some extent which species is being sought, a single four- to six-foot piece of monofilament or fluorocarbon in twelve- to thirty-pound test will suffice for many situations.

To attach, tie a Double Surgeon's Loop at one end of the mono leader and attach to the loop at the end of the shooting head. Then tie the fly to the other end of the mono leader.

This is a simple and effective way of keeping your fly in the zone and getting more strikes.

16

How to make a redfish leader: the Half and Half

THE REDFISH IS AN OUTSTANDING FISH ON THE FLY. It's aggressive and strong, and provides the chance to experience outstanding sight-casting. This fish is not as spooky as the bonefish or tarpon, so the leader system can be very simple.

The Half and Half is a nine-foot, two-part leader system that is easy to make and casts well. The butt section should be a thirty- or forty-pound test, four-and-a-half- to five-foot piece of monofilament; attach it to a twenty-pound piece of mono, of similar length, with a Blood Knot.

In most situations, this is all you will need.

The Half and Half is the ideal redfish leader.

17

Creating a loop on the end of your fly line

THE ARE MANY WAYS TO ATTACH YOUR FLY LINE to your leader. Many fly lines come with a premade loop on the end; unfortunately, these loops tend to pull apart when subjected to heavy pressure.

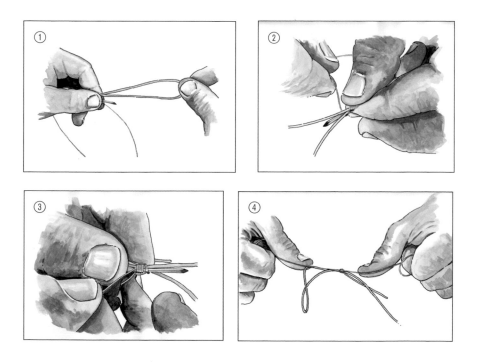

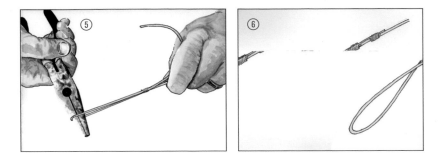

To tie your own, begin by forming a strong, whip-finished loop at the end of your fly line. If properly formed, the loop will exceed your fly line's strength.

1. Fold over the end of the fly line and double the line.
2. Make the loop large enough to allow a fly to pass through it.
3. Tie three Nail Knots on the doubled-up part of the fly line.
4. Secure the Nail Knots, then test them by securing the loop around a dull object like the end of a pair of pliers and applying tension on the loop.
5. A coating of Super Glue or Knot Sense on each Nail Knot will ensure that the knots will hold and not unravel during a prolonged fight with a gamefish.

18

Attaching the leader to the sinking line

MOST SINKING LINES CONTAIN A MONOCORE (coated monofilament core). These lines are strong and able to handle the demands placed upon them by hard-fighting saltwater gamefish.

These lines do have a weakness, however, in that an incorrect connection between the leader and the line, such as a Nail Knot, can cause the monocore's coating to strip off while you are fighting a fish.

A better option is the Albright Knot. It's bulky, but it's a very solid and reliable choice.

Even better, don't use a knot at all, but put a loop in the end of your sinking line. Take fifteen-pound monofilament and use two Nail Knots to create a loop in the end of the sinking line. Once the loop is made, coat the Nail Knots with Knot Sense or some other glue. If done properly, this loop will not break.

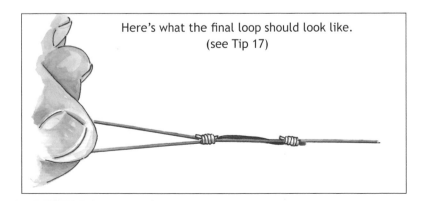

Here's what the final loop should look like.
(see Tip 17)

19

How to tie a Bimini Twist

THE BIMINI TWIST IS AN IMPORTANT SALTWATER knot that you should know how to tie. It has a high breaking strength and can be used for a variety of connections, from IGFA tippets to mono shock tippets, or even connecting mono to steel leaders.

The Bimini requires practice to master, but once you understand the process, you'll find it to be a very useful knot that you'll come to rely upon in a variety of situations. Follow these eight steps:

1. Form a loop in the line. Place one hand in the bottom of the loop and make twenty to twenty-five twists by rotating your hand.
2. Place the loop around your foot; then, with both hands, pull the two ends of the line apart, twisting the line into tight spirals.
3. Take the tag end of the line and, at a right angle, let it spin downward toward your foot. Pull up lightly on the line, letting the tag end roll down toward the loop.
4. Work the tag end all the way down to the top of the loop.
5. Hold the wraps tightly, make a Half Hitch on one side of the loop, then pull tight, which will secure all the downward wraps.
6. Take the tag end and make four to six Half Hitches around both legs of the loop.
7. Pull the tag and force all the wraps together.

8. Finally, place the loop around a boat cleat or something equally secure and pull the knot together. Trim the tag ends.

Master the Bimini Twist and you'll not only impress your fishing buddies with your tying skills, but you'll also be using one of the most important and secure knots associated with saltwater fly fishing.

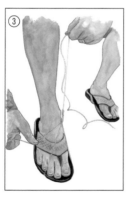
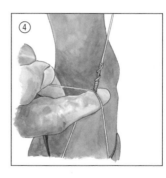
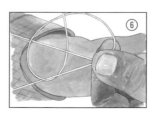
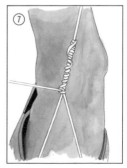
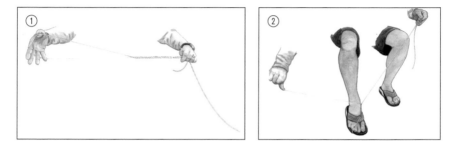
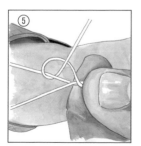

20

How to tie a Figure Eight Loop knot using soft stainless steel wire

SOFT STAINLESS WIRE IS A GOOD ALTERNATIVE TO single-strand wire. It works well on the smaller saltwater gamefish, such as the Pacific barracuda and bonito, which the fly rodder will encounter in many nearshore fisheries.

The best attribute of the soft stainless wire is that you can tie a loop knot in it, thus avoiding the time-consuming process of making the Haywire Twist that is so commonly used with single-strand wire.

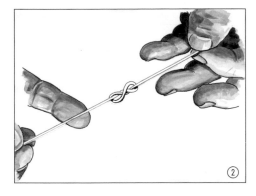

②

③

④

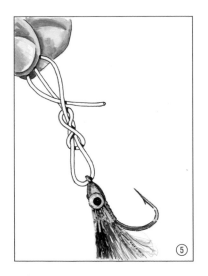

⑤

⑥

21

Coat fishing knots with Knot Sense

WHEN YOU'RE FIGHTING A SALTWATER GAMEFISH, your leader system is sorely tested as the fish makes long, strong runs along mangrove shoots, coral heads, and rock pinnacles. There are times when it's impossible to avoid breaking off a fish; however, one way to make certain your knots can stand the stress of a long battle is to coat them with Knot Sense, a liquid that will strengthen your connections and smooth out your tag ends.

Knot Sense is a clear liquid with the consistency of household dish soap. Because it solidifies when exposed to the sun's rays, it should be applied outdoors or in direct sunlight; once dried, it creates a clear, soft coating around your leader connections. While setting, the liquid penetrates the knot's wraps, helping bond them into stronger and more dependable links.

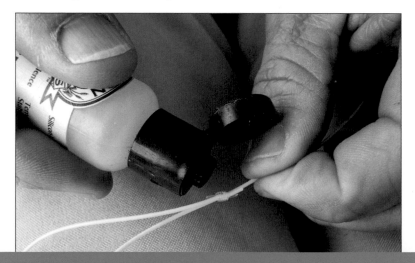

22

Reading a fish finder or GPS

IF YOU'RE A BOAT OWNER AND YOU FLY-FISH IN SALT-water, at some point you'll have to read a fish finder or a global positioning system (GPS) unit. The fish finder/GPS unit is a key component to success when fishing the salt. Whether pinpointing schools of baitfish, locating structure, reading water temperatures, or getting safely back to your launching site, this unit's importance to the angler cannot be over-stated. Some portable models can even be mounted on a kayak. Tackle stores and mail-order and online cata-logs stock a wide variety of units; all share similar fea-tures, the most important being the following:

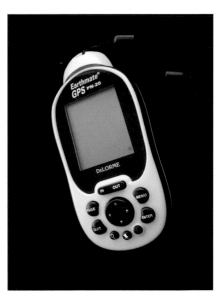

1. GPS for navigation
2. Water temperature
3. Bathymetry (locating un-derwater structure)
4. Sonar for locating baitfish and gamefish

23

Don't forget the long-nosed pliers

I CAN'T REMEMBER HOW MANY TIMES I'VE BROUGHT a barracuda, shark, or bluefish in to be released, only to realize I had only short-nosed pliers with which to remove the hook from the fish's mouth. Short-nosed pliers work well enough for freshwater fishing, but for dealing with the teeth of many saltwater gamefish, the wise angler carries long-nosed pliers. To paraphrase an old TV commercial, "Don't leave home without them."

There are two important reasons for packing these fishing aids: First, they protect your fingers, for even the smallest barracuda can take a nasty bite out of your finger, while a bluefish has the potential to sink its razor-sharp teeth clear to the bone. Furthermore, if the fish is deeply hooked in the throat, the long-nosed pliers will give you a better chance of removing the hook and releasing the fish unharmed.

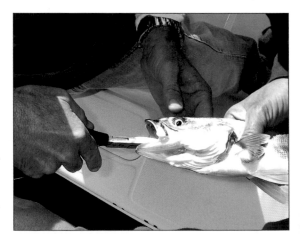

Long-nosed pliers are useful for ▶ extracting hooks.

24

Use a net in salt water

THE FISH NET IS NOT JUST FOR STREAM OR LAKE fishing; it's also a useful aid in safely catching and releasing saltwater gamefish. It helps you control a fish, remove the hook from its tooth-filled mouth, and then release it without causing it harm.

If you are a catch-and-release fly fisherman, employing a net is easier on the fish once it is brought to boat or shore. Handling the fish can be harmful to it, as your hands tend to remove the fish's protective slime coating, leaving it susceptible to bacterial and fungal infection after it's released.

The standard trout net may be a bit small, but there are many great medium to large nets on the market. Select a net that suits the fishing you have planned. Smaller nets are suitable for Southern California's surf perch and corbina; larger nets are needed for tackling species such as Gulf Coast redfish or East Coast stripers. Use only nets that have black rubberlike webbing, as the soft, slick texture will not harm the fish. Forget about using grandpa's old aluminum net with the green polypropylene webbing. These nets do the fish more harm than good.

Using a net can help tame an unwieldy gamefish. ▶

25

Polarized sunglasses

WHETHER YOU'RE STALKING BONEFISH ON THE flats or sight-casting to tuna offshore, your most important piece of equipment, next to the fly reel, is quality polarized sunglasses, which eliminate glare from the water's surface. Drugstore sunglasses? Forget them. All they do is make you look sharp. A pair of high-end polarized glasses is well worth the money.

The variety of polarized lens color choices can be confusing, so here are a few guidelines in selecting your glasses:

1. For shallow flats, beaches, and marshes: amber lenses
2. For deep water, offshore waters, and bright sunlight: gray lenses
3. For softer light, glare, and cloudy days: yellow, light rose, or amber lenses

Frame styles vary greatly, but function and coverage are the major concerns. Choose a frame that provides good coverage over the eyes, as well as in the temple area. Look for frames that do not let in light peripherally (from the side of the head), and choose a frame that will remain comfortable throughout a long day of fishing. Consider lightweight frames with arms that don't pinch behind the ears.

In the past, most anglers chose glass as a lens material. Glass is durable and relatively scratch-resistant, although it's heavy. Nowadays, outstanding synthetic lens materials such as polycarbonate and SR-91 are good alternative choices. SR-91 is strong, light, and has superior light transmission and clarity. Wearing glasses with SR-91 lenses all day isn't as much of a burden on your nose.

Eyewear is a personal choice. Whether you're a hipster or lean more toward the traditional styles, the important things to remember are lens coloration and eye coverage. Oh, and don't forget a lanyard for your glasses. It would be a shame to lose your expensive pair of shades to the deep blue sea!

Good polarized sunglasses will help you pinpoint more fish.

26

Proper footwear for fishing

IF I COULD FISH BAREFOOT, I WOULD; HOWEVER, THIS is not practical in many saltwater situations. A good pair of fishing shoes is as important as your favorite fishing hat, shirt, or sunglasses. It's important that your feet are properly shod for any occasion.

On the Skiff

When skiff fishing, a firm-soled running or deck shoe works well, but with modifications. The first thing I do when I put on a pair is to tuck in the laces snugly, leaving no exposed dangling ends. Fly lines can hang up on anything, but loose laces always seem to be at the top of the list. I know some fly fishers who are so concerned with this problem that they run duct tape around their shoes to keep the laces covered. And don't forget: No black soles!

Sandals? I would leave them at home. Like shoelaces, the straps on sandals pose another problem in line hangup.

Flip-flops, if you are so inclined, are an acceptable and comfortable option, as they have no line-grabbing laces or straps. On the downside, they offer little support for your feet.

On the Beach and Flats

There are hundreds of different types of practical shoes that will fit your needs on fishing trips. Select a shoe with high ankle support, a firm and solid toe, and stiff arch support. Since you'll be wading in a variety of bottom conditions, including mud, soft sand, hard sand, and even coral reefs, select a shoe that has a thick sole to prevent punctures. If you fish with a stripping basket, you can use sandals because there is less chance of your line getting snagged on the straps of the conventional wading shoe.

Rocks and Jetties

If you fish from rocks and jetties, heavy-duty wading boots are not only comfortable, but provide great support. If you choose not to wear waders, then wear two pairs of socks in the boots for a better fit.

Proper footwear protects your feet when walking on coral reefs.

27

The stripping basket

WHEN FISHING FROM THE BEACH, THERE IS NOTHING more frustrating than having your fly line wrap and tangle around your legs and feet, especially after you have just made a perfect cast to a school of gamefish.

The simplest way to solve this problem is to invest in a stripping basket. Made from a variety of materials and available in many styles, the stripping basket will assist you in managing your line, leaving you free to concentrate on improving your casting and distance.

The stripping basket is not limited to beach fishing. More and more anglers are also accepting the value of the stripping basket on boats. This taller, free-standing cousin to the standard wearable basket allows you to keep your line off the deck and avoid potential hangups with boat cleats, shoelaces, coolers, and other obstacles commonly found on a boat deck.

A large stripping basket on the bow of a
skiff helps you avoid tangles and add distance to your casts.

28

Wear a wading belt when fishing the surf

THE SURF ZONE CAN BE LIKENED TO A ROUGH NEIGH-borhood, an environment where you must exercise great caution. There are a few things that you can do to ensure your safety, how-ever.

Since most of us wear waders when fly fishing the surf, it is important to use a wading belt, a seemingly unimportant piece of equipment that could save your life if you are lifted up and thrown into the drink by a large breaker. In the surf zone, it also isn't uncommon to have your feet swept out from under you by a rip current, leaving you in a helpless position. Even if you're a swimmer with the talent of an Olympic gold medalist, once your beltless waders fill up with water, you'll find it almost impossible to regain your footing. Without that belt tightly cinched around your middle, you are a candidate for the morning paper's obits.

The tightened wader belt creates a nice pocket of air below your waist, giving you a little buoyancy as well as saving you the problem of dealing with the extra weight of full-to-the-brim waders. To be most effective, the belt should be positioned above your hips.

For added safety, some fly fishers also wear an inflatable life vest, especially if they are not good swimmers. Most vests can be inflated with the pull of a string; many come equipped with pockets for storing fly boxes and other gear.

No matter what you wear, always remember this: Never turn your back to the surf.

A wading belt should always be worn while fishing the surf.

PART
3

Casting

29

The double haul

MANY BEGINNING SALTWATER FLY ANGLERS WILL invest a ton of money buying the best equipment, and spend thousands of dollars traveling to exotic locations that offer incredible fishing for the likes of trophy tarpon or permit. Then, once they are on the bow of the boat, ready to cast to the fish of a lifetime, they're unable to cast the fly into the wind or achieve the distance required to reach the fish—a situation that is frustrating not only to the angler, but to the guide as well. The key to solving this problem is to learn to double haul: It will improve your casting speed and accuracy, enable you to cast the fly into the wind, and let you cast a weighted shooting head or sinking line. The end result is that you'll catch more fish. And you know what? The double haul is easier to learn than you might think.

Start by finding an open, grassy area (parks are great places to work on your casting, but watch for kids and dogs). Strip off forty feet of fly line, make a single forward cast, and lay out the line in front of you. Now, with the rod tip on the grass, pick up the fly line and make a backcast. Let it unfurl and lie behind you on the grass. This is a single haul.

Once the fly line is laid out behind, make a forward cast by pulling the line off the lawn with your line hand while your rod

①

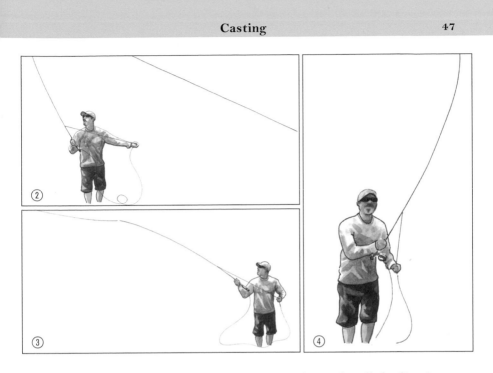

is moving forward. As you bring your rod forward, pull the line in your hand down toward your waist. You will feel the rod load up as it bends, and then the line will shoot forward. Release the line from your hand as it starts to go forward, and watch it fly forward through the guides. This is what gives you the extra distance and lets you push through the wind. This is the second or double haul.

Once you get the feel of both the single and double haul, keep the forward and backcasts off the lawn. You should be able to feel the line accelerating on both the backcast and forward cast.

30

Develop a good backcast

BEING ABLE TO LAY OUT THIRTY OR FORTY FEET OF fly line behind you is a skill you need to master. Fish can materialize behind you as easily as they can in front of you, and a quick, accurate backcast will improve your chances of catching them.

You can make the backcast in the same manner as the forward cast. First make a forward cast, allowing the line to lie on the water, then pick up the line and shoot it behind you. This move is called the water haul (see Tip 32); instead of coming forward with the forward cast, you now allow the fly line to lay out behind you in the area where you spotted the fish. You can proceed with stripping the line from there, just as you would if the fish were in front of you.

31

The Long Cast

FOR ALL INTENTS AND PURPOSES, THE HUNDRED-
foot cast does not exist in fly fishing. There has been much lore and
myth around the need to make the "hundred-footer" to saltwater
fish. Even if an angler were able to make such a long cast, seeing the
take and successfully hooking a fish from that distance is extremely
difficult.

A more realistic casting expectation for all fly anglers is the ability
to cast fifty feet quickly and with minimal false casting. The sooner
the fly is in the water and not in the air, the more chances you're
going to have to catch the fish. False casting will often spook the fish,
and then it won't matter how far you can cast . . . the fish is gone.

A quick, accurate, fifty-foot cast will cover most saltwater situations.

32

The water haul

IN MANY SITUATIONS, LONG (FIFTY-PLUS FEET), accurate double hauls are required if you want to catch fish. But what happens when you're casting to fish in deep water? Or casting into the shore break as the currents from the waves are dragging your line back and forth? How about casting a 550- or 650-grain shooting head or sinking line from a tossing and pitching boat on the open ocean? This is not the place for artful double hauling. This is rock and roll fly fishing, and the name of the game here is to get the fly quickly into the water so you can catch fish.

When you're using a heavy sinking line, the water haul is usually the most practical cast. Here is how to do it:

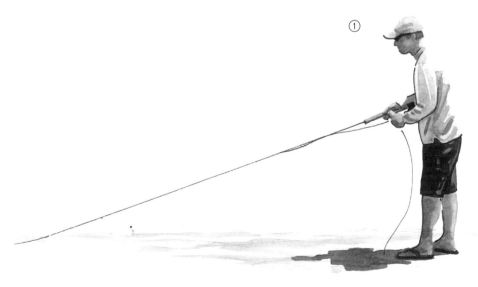

1. Make your forward cast at a comfortable distance.
2. Once the cast is out in front of you, with the rod tip on the water, strip the line in until you get the sinking part of the shooting head at the tip of your rod.
3. Slowly lift up your rod tip and make a roll cast. This will lay the line out straight in front of you.
4. Now make a slow backcast and feel the line drag up off the water.
5. Let the sinking line fall out behind you on the water as if you were presenting a fly to a fish behind you.
6. Once the line is laid out behind you, make a forward cast and pull the line with your free hand with a downstroke toward your hip, then release the line.

   The resistance of the water (the haul) on both the forward cast and backcast will create enough friction and drag to project the fly line forward, acting as a double haul without any false casting.

   The water haul is also a great way to master the double haul.

33

Flip cast

IF YOU LIKE TO SIGHT-CAST TO FISH CRUISING THE beach or flats, it's critical to learn the flip cast or "quick cast." This is a cast that may measure only a few feet, but it's good to know for those times when fish suddenly materialize at close range. Making a good flip cast, so you can quickly place the fly in the fish's hit zone, can make the difference between hooking your quarry or not.

Start by laying out thirty to fifty feet of line, then strip it in, leaving the last twenty-five feet of the fly line (and belly section) outside the rod tip. This will allow you to load the rod during the cast, thus minimizing false casting. Place the fly in the palm of your off hand (the hand not holding the rod) or between your thumb and index finger.

When a fish swims within range—and remember, many fish will approach within twenty feet— make your backcast while releasing the fly from your hand, then cast to the fish. If the fish is behind you, your backcast may actually be the cast you make to the fish. Don't make any false casts, if possible.

◀ Hold the fly between your thumb and index finger.

34

Casting into a crosswind

THROWING A FLY IN A CROSSWIND OR A FOLLOWING wind off your casting arm's shoulder is perhaps fly fishing's most troublesome cast. I have seen many casts blown and fish missed because of an angler's failure to properly execute this cast. No matter where you fish in the salt, you will, at some point, be tested by a crosswind or following wind.

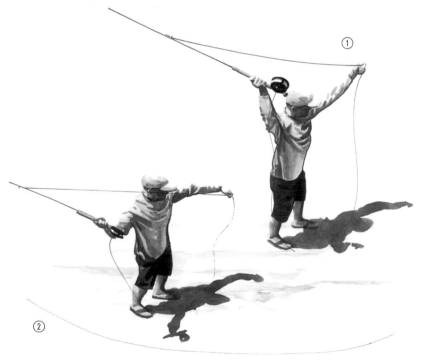

When you're placed in this trying situation, the Belgian or heli-copter cast is your most effective cast. This cast should be executed quickly, with a minimum of backcasts. When winds become erratic and disagreeable, as is their habit on salt water, this cast can be the great equalizer to a seemingly insoluble problem.

To do it, first make a high backcast; then, make your forward cast a high overhead cast (liken your casting arm to a helicopter's blade as you make the transition from side cast to forward overhead cast).

With practice, you can easily master this cast. Whether you are fishing on the flats, the beach, or the open ocean, it will give you confidence when you find yourself dealing with winds.

Techniques

35

Blend into your environment

YOU'VE PROBABLY SEEN PICTURES OF A GUY WEARING a bright red shirt and yellow shorts, holding a good-size bonefish. This outfit might make for a pretty photo, and it may be okay for Mardi Gras, but it's terrible for fishing. When you're trying to be stealthy, a brightly colored fishing outfit will send fish darting for cover.

Blend into your environment. Match your clothes to your surroundings. If you are fishing the beach, wear neutral colors such as tan, light green, or even brown. For fishing the flats, a light blue shirt and stone-colored shorts or pants are your best choices. And don't overlook camouflage outfits when stalking spooky fish in shallow water. There are plenty of camouflage patterns on today's market that allow you to blend into the environment, giving you a decided advantage in fly fishing the marshes and backwaters.

A stealthy approach starts with the correct clothes.

36

The boat as a clock

IMAGINE A CLOCK LYING ON ITS BACK. ACCORDING to my father, a World War II veteran, the United States Army Air Force used it as a directional system to help gunners pick up the positions of attacking enemy fighter aircraft. Now imagine your boat as a flat clock, its numerals used by your guide to direct your attention to a fish's position and where to aim your cast. Think of the bow as twelve o'clock, starboard as three o'clock, the stern as six o'clock, and port as nine o'clock. Understanding this system will contribute to your success in taking more fish, making your fly fishing more productive and pleasurable.

My analogy may seem a bit farfetched, but as you progress as a saltwater fly angler, you will eventually hire a guide who will not only captain your boat but will also be a great source of information and suggestions. Almost all guides employ the clock system: When he says, "Tarpon at ten o'clock," you need to understand what he is saying and why, so you can act accordingly.

37

Learn how to clear your fly line

HOOKING A FISH ON FLY GEAR IS SOMETIMES THE easiest part of the game; what happens after the fish is hooked is probably more important. Nothing can demonstrate this more than clearing your fly line after a fish has been hooked. This is what I call the "hero to zero in three seconds."

Here is the scenario: You make a fifty-foot cast to a school of tuna, a tailing bonefish, or a string of tarpon. You begin stripping your fly back toward you, trying to snooker a fish into striking. A fish follows the fly to within a few feet of the boat, then strikes. You set the hook, and you're tight to the fish. The fish makes a lightning-fast run away from the boat. You look down and discover you've got a large pile of fly line at your feet. Now what?

First, transfer your thinking from the fish to the line—easier said than done. Let the fish run. He's hooked, and if you keep tension on him, he'll stay that way. Do not lift your rod tip; keep the rod angled at ninety degrees.

Do not hold the fly line. This will result in a broken tippet.

Now, focus on clearing the line at your feet while keeping a light grip on the line with your thumb and index finger. Allow line to run through your fingers until the line is tight to the reel. This may seem to take forever, but it will actually take only a few seconds.

If you notice a knot while clearing your line, do not attempt to undo it; instead, allow it to travel through the guides. In most cases the knot will not hinder the line-clearing process. You can deal with it later.

Once the fly line is on the reel, apply positive tension and begin fighting the fish.

Proper clearing of the line can make the difference between landing and losing a fish.

38

Coils in your fly line

COILS IN A FLY LINE ARE A BAD THING. THEY AFFECT your casting; plus, they are more than likely to foul and hang up in a rod guide during a fight, often resulting in a lost fish, a broken tippet, or worse, a snapped rod tip. Regularly stretching your fly line can eliminate this problem.

Perhaps the simplest way to stretch a line is to strip out the length you'll need in a particular circumstance. Place the line beneath your foot, form a loop, and securely hold it about waist high. Then give the line a solid, steady pull, applying tension on the line between your hand and your foot. Repeat this process until the entire line has been stretched, and all the coils have been removed.

During the course of a day on the water, keep your line stretched by repeating this procedure every time you notice that coils are forming.

39

Don't take your eyes off the water

ON MORE THAN ONE OCCASION, WHILE FISHING A shallow flat for redfish or laying out a chum line for sharks, I have allowed my eyes to drift off the water for a split second, and in that brief period missed an opportunity to make a good fly presentation to the fish of a lifetime. Rushed, I made a sloppy cast and spooked my quarry.

When you're sight-casting, it's critical to keep your eyes riveted on the water, no matter how difficult it can be after hours spent squinty-eyed, looking for fish and finding none. Be visually disciplined! Be focused! For the minute you take your eyes off the water, that trophy fish will come finning into casting range.

If you are fly fishing at the beach, it's equally important to keep an eye on the surf. Waves may hit a lull, your focus drifts, and then a new set of waves sneaks up on you when you least expect it. You may not only lose your gear and end up soaking wet, but if you are precariously perched on some rocks, you could be swept into the water—a dangerous situation, to say the least.

Focus!

40

How to hook fish that follow your fly all the way to the rod tip

IT'S VERY FRUSTRATING WHEN A GAMEFISH FOL-lows your fly practically to the rod tip, but refuses to strike. There is, however, an easy way to get a picky fish to take your offering. I call it "sweeping the fly."

When a fish has followed the fly to within a few feet of your rod tip (usually you'll have five to ten feet of line outside the tip), lower

your rod tip and make a sweeping motion as if you were going to make a sidearm back-cast. Don't pull the fly out of the water—just keep it moving. On the sweep, the fly will move smoothly through the water, doing a great impersonation of a fidgety baitfish attempting to escape a predator. This move enjoys a high percentage of success. The trick is to exercise control over your emotions and not to pull the fly from the fish's mouth if it strikes. The hook-set is always very close to you, so be prepared to let the fish run, which means managing the line as it shoots through the guides.

41

Fly-fish from a kayak

THE KAYAK IS A STEALTHY AND EFFECTIVE VEHICLE to use for fly fishing, a means to access fishing areas where fish are normally easily spooked, such as flats, marshes, and kelp beds. In addition, a kayak is not only portable, but it requires a smaller investment than a flats skiff and is more environmentally friendly (no gasoline or motor oil required).

The kayak is an affordable way to explore backcountry waters.

A properly equipped kayak can store a couple of fly rods, fly boxes, a BogaGrip (for holding fish by the lip, for hook removal), and even a push pole.

Using a kayak, you can stand and sight-cast on shallow flats, or paddle offshore to the kelp beds. If you feel uncomfortable paddling with a double-bladed paddle, then a pedal kayak may be more to your taste and abilities. Yet another option is a kayak with a small, battery-operated trolling motor, which lets you cover more water and even work into the wind.

On a kayak, the fly line can be stripped right onto the deck without your having to worry about hanging up on boat cleats or other obstacles.

A sea anchor will help you stay in position if you're fishing structure or around kelp beds. On the flats, a small anchor can help keep you in one spot.

If you do opt for a kayak, consider using a longer fly rod, preferably a nine and a half-footer. A rod this long will help keep your line off the water on your backcast and enable you to make longer casts.

42

Stand-up paddleboard? Why not?

ONE OF THE HOTTEST NEW METHODS OF ANGLING for saltwater fish on the fly rod is from a stand-up paddleboard (SUP). Southern California fishermen have been fishing off their surfboards for years, but the recent SUP rage has created all sorts of venues for the more progressive saltwater fly fisher. Besides providing easier portability, the paddleboard gives you a better platform from which to spot, sneak up on, and cast to fish.

The SUP is an extremely versatile fishing platform, a craft you can launch anywhere, and all you need for transport is a cartop rack or a pickup truck. Much lighter than a kayak, the SUP is at home in shallow waters inaccessible by boat or in deepwater areas not frequented by the general public (simply toss it into a boat and take it where you want to go).

Outfit the SUP the same as you would a kayak, using a fishing box specifically designed for fly fishing, with a rod holder and places for your paddle, fly box, and other tackle. You can also build one to your own specifications.

If you use an SUP on a regular basis, you'll notice that your waistline will benefit. Paddling an SUP, whether kneeling or standing, is a great workout. Cancel that gym membership. Now you've got another excuse to go fishing . . . you're exercising!

As with kayak fishing, it takes some time to master the art of SUP fly fishing. You have to keep in mind, for example, that you will be pushed by the wind, so you need to be aware of your drift and compensate accordingly. Calm, glassy waters are best for the SUP, but offshore is not out of the question. In time, you'll really come to appreciate the benefits of an SUP.

The SUP allows for better sight casting than a sit-in kayak.

43

How to avoid cutting your fingers on the fly line: gaffer's tape

SALTWATER IS HARD ON FINGERS AND TENDS TO produce painful cuts, especially in your index finger, in just a few hours on the water. To counter this, buy gaffer's tape, available at any hardware store, and wrap your digits before you go fishing.

The tape has an adhesive that binds together after it is wrapped around your fingers and can be worn the entire day without replacement. Wrap your index, middle, and third fingers on your rod hand, as they take the brunt of stripping line. It's not a bad idea to protect all your fingers, for that matter.

Cut fingers can ruin your day. Protect them with gaffer's' tape. ▶

44

Know your birds

IN FISHING, THERE ARE MANY VISUAL INDICATIONS
that fish are on the bite. One of the easiest and most reliable signs
to identify is bird activity.

Keep an eye on bird activity.

Some species of birds are better indicators than others, and you don't have to be an ornithologist to recognize the better ones; a basic knowledge of the bird kingdom will do. Let's look at the birds and how they rate in priority and importance to successful fish finding.

The best fish-locating birds of all, terns work diligently in searching for baitfish. If you spot them picking and fluttering in an area, that's a good sign that gamefish are working baitfish. Terns often fly ahead of a school of gamefish, picking up baitfish that have been pushed to the surface.

Pelicans: The big daddies of the seabird world. Though not as agile and swift as terns, pelicans will tell you where the main bodies of baitfish and gamefish are. Pelicans will dive with abandon into the center of a bait ball, filling their mouths with as many baitfish as possible. By habit, pelicans will not allow a bait ball to relocate too far from them. So if you spot a pelican positioned on the water, you can be sure that bait and gamefish are in the area.

Gulls are the scavengers of the sea. Seagulls are opportunistic feeders that will feed on anything, from popcorn to anchovies. Their presence is a good sign that baitfish are about, but they can hoodwink even the best fisherman by diving on anything they can eat, including everything from plastic bottle caps to sardines. Keep that in mind when turning to gulls to find fish.

45

Line management

ONE SURE WAY TO LOSE A FISH IS THROUGH POOR line management. The line, often coiled at the angler's feet during a hookup, will fly uncontrollably off the deck and through the guides as the fish makes its run for safety. This is the moment when line management is essential. If the fly line is brought tight once the fish has begun its run, the battle is half won. However, if loose fly line jumps off the deck and wraps around the angler's shoe, leg, boat bag, or whatever happens to be lying loose on the deck, it is quite possible that the line will come tight and the leader will break, resulting in a lost fish.

Losing fish in this manner happens to even the best saltwater fly anglers. The secret is to fish with a stripping basket or bucket. Not only will a stripping basket keep your fly line neatly coiled off the boat's deck, away from any obstructions; it will also keep it clean of sand, grit, mud, and grime.

◄ Proper line management is essential for successful fishing.

46

How to retrieve a saltwater fly

Baitfish

IF YOU ARE USING A FLY THAT IMITATES THE MOVE-
ments of a baitfish, try to observe the behavior patterns of the
actual baitfish. How fast are they swimming? Are they swimming
in schools or small groups when being chased by gamefish? Are
they stunned by gamefish before being eaten as they are sinking
or, in fishing lingo, "on the fall"? Most injured baitfish swim in
frenzied motions, so quick, short retrieves are generally the best. In

Think like a baitfish.

conditions where the baitfish are lazily swimming about, try slower, longer strips to get your adversaries' attention.

Baitfish always swim into the current, so when fishing from a drifting boat, cast your fly upcurrent, then let it sink and drift in the current. At the end of the drift, as the fly swings behind the boat, allow it to gyrate, lifelike, in the current for a few seconds before beginning stripping. This technique often results in a strike, so hang on!

Crabs or Shrimp

If you're attempting to imitate a crab or shrimp, make short, small strips so the fly looks like it's scurrying along. This move usually gets a fish's attention. If you spot a gamefish eyeing the fly and beginning to approach it, stop stripping and allow the fly to sit motionless. Wait a few seconds, move it again in short spurts, and get ready!

47

The best rod angle for fighting fish on the flats or in shallow water

IN TROUT FISHING, WE ARE TAUGHT TO KEEP THE rod high while fighting a fish. This accomplishes two things: First, it protects the light tippet, and second, it keeps the fish's head up, preventing it from moving into the current or deeper water. In saltwater fly fishing, however, we are using heavy, strong tippets that are virtually impossible to break, and enable you to exert maximum pressure when fighting a fish. To do this, employ a low rod angle and use the rod's butt section to do the fighting for you. When you're hooked up to a saltwater fish in shallow water, the higher the rod angle, the less pressure you put on the fish. Lowering the rod's angle will allow you to use the fly rod's butt section, allowing for more pressure on the fish.

◀ Use a low rod angle for maximum pressure when fighting fish in shallow water.

48

Securing your fly to the stripping guide

MANY FLY FISHERMEN PAY LITTLE OR NO ATTENTION to securing the fly to the rod, a simple procedure that you should do automatically. When your fly is always secured in the same place, with no slack line, you can get to it quickly, without thinking, in case you have to make a split-second cast. This can prove the difference between a fish caught and a cast wasted.

Traditional hook keepers at the butt end of the fly rod, right above the handle, work well for securing your hook between casts or while the rod is in a holder. However, I find that if you pass the line around the reel seat and secure your fly to the first, second, or third stripping guide, you have a few more feet of fly line out of the rod tip, making it much easier to make a quick cast without having to strip any line off the fly reel. Remember, saltwater fly fishing can be a quick-fire, shoot-from-the-hip

game; having a few extra feet of fly line extending outside the tip of your fly rod may mean the difference between success or failure.

One word of caution: Don't put the hook directly inside the guide. Instead, use the rod guide's leg bracing to hold the hook—a hook positioned inside a guide may damage the fragile ceramic ring.

49

The short stroke

IF YOU HAVE SPENT ANY TIME FISHING ON CHARTER boats, you have observed that the best anglers always bring their fish to gaff with as little fanfare as possible. These guys move fluidly, keeping constant pressure on the fish as it takes them around the boat, all with the intention of bringing in that fish quickly. You may also have noticed that they dig the rod tip deep in the water as they reel in line, each dig followed by a short lift of the rod tip, pulling the fish up from the depths. This technique is called the "short

Always apply maximum pressure when short-stroking fish.

stroke," and fly fishermen can use it as well. There are four key elements to the technique.

1. Keep your shoulders square to the fish at all times. If your shoulders are not square, you lose leverage when lifting the fish from the depths.

2. Keep the rod tip pointed down at the fish, a move that will prevent you from bringing your rod up too high. Any rod angle higher than ninety degrees is of little help when fighting a bluewater gamefish with a fly rod. The fly rod is designed to fight fish from the butt end. Raising it above ninety degrees shifts the fighting energy from the butt to the weaker midsection and tip section, and that should never happen.

3. When you're bringing up a fish from deep water and the fish takes a break, put on the heat. Never let the fish rest. Always try to keep it moving up toward the surface. Break the fish as soon as you can.

4. Finally, when bringing a fish out of deep water, make short pumps of the rod while retrieving line as the rod tip drops.

50

Shuffle your feet while walking the flats or beach

THERE IS NOTHING MORE EXCRUCIATING THAN being stung by a ray while you are walking the flats or beach. These injuries are not only painful, but if not treated quickly and properly, they can turn into serious health problems.

Beware the barbed tail!

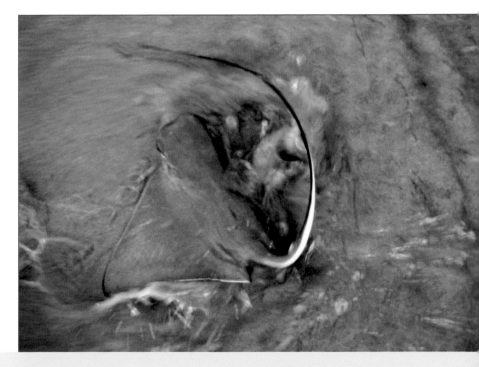

Even if you are wearing neoprene wading booties or flats boots, you are not totally protected from having a ray's barbed spike penetrate your foot or ankle. I've had that filth-encrusted spike poke through my boot and puncture my foot right to the bone! The sting was bad enough, but the painful throbbing that followed had me on the verge of tears.

The ray's stinger is sharp and pointed, and loaded with potentially infectious bacteria. Rays live on the shallow flats and surf zones, burying themselves in the sand for protection and camouflage, and if startled or stepped on, they swing their spiked tails in defense.

If you are fly fishing in the surf or the flats, shuffle your feet, pushing sand as you walk cautiously along the sandy bottom. If you have to pick up your feet, do it slowly and look down before placing them back on the sand. Shuffling also sends out warning signals to rays. They can feel the vibrations of your feet shuffling through the water and will swim away. Of course, you don't want to spook your prey with the same movements, so shuffle slowly and cautiously.

51

Adding depth to a sinking fly—the hit zone

WHEN FISHING IN DEEP WATER FOR SPECIES SUCH as stripers, tuna, bonito, yellowtail, or amberjacks, it is critical to get your fly to the correct depth in the water column. The hit zone can be just a few feet below the surface or as deep as thirty feet.

The proper depth can produce big fish.

A sinking line or shooting head is the accepted way of getting the fly into the zone, but there are other ways of adding more depth.

From a Drifting Boat

Position yourself in the bow or stern and cast upcurrent, or in the direction the boat is drifting. As the boat drifts, the fly will sink deeper. When the line is directly in front of you and comes taut, begin stripping in the fly.

From an Anchored Boat

The upcurrent cast works just as well from an anchored boat. This method has an advantage over the drifting boat in that the fly will sink deeper because the boat is not moving. This approach is especially effective if you're fishing around deepwater rocks, pilings, and offshore oil rigs.

From the Shore or Jetty

Thinking of swinging a fly for salmon or steelhead? The previously mentioned techniques are just as effective in sinking your fly from the beach or jetty. Determine the direction of the current or rip. Cast the fly up into the current and allow the fly and line to swing past you until the line tightens; now, begin your retrieve. Remember that many strikes occur as your fly is sinking or on the swing, so be alert for subtle and out-of-the-ordinary movements of your line.

52

Bow to a tarpon

THE SIGHT OF A TARPON JUMPING AND TWISTING and gyrating in the air, in an attempt to dislodge a fly from its mouth, is an absolutely jaw-dropping experience. Few fish rival the strength and acrobatics that this great gamefish brings to saltwater fly fishing.

Once hooked, a tarpon's first reaction is to run for cover, then make numerous rod-jolting jumps as it attempts to rid its mouth of the annoying hook. Since tarpon are hooked at relatively close range, it's important that the angler point his fly rod directly at the fish the moment it makes its initial leap. This move, called "bowing," puts slack in the line, creating a shock absorber for the tippet. If the angler is unprepared and fails to bow, the tarpon will hightail it away from the boat, causing extreme pressure on the tippet, which often results in a broken leader and a lost fish.

To avoid this problem, the angler must anticipate when the tarpon will jump—not an easy task but one a successful tarpon angler must master. Another way to anticipate the jump is to listen to the sound of the reel's drag during the fish's run; when the sound reaches an ear-torturing howl, be ready, as the jump is about to happen.

Treat the
tarpon like a
king—BOW!

53

How to tip and roll a fish

TIPPING IS SOMETHING YOU DO AFTER A GREAT meal at a restaurant. In the case of saltwater fly fishing, however, it's what the angler does toward the end of a fight with a big gamefish. When a large gamefish makes a run directly in front of the angler and there is no good angle to let him apply pressure to move the fish's head and make him change direction, smart anglers do something called "tipping the fish." To do this, the angler tips his fly rod upside down, lowers the tip into the water, and applies pressure from under the surface. This pressure will in most cases stop the fish and roll him over.

Once the fish has rolled over, the angler can retrieve line while moving close to the fish (on foot or in a boat). Oftentimes the fish will concede for a short period, which will give the angler time to regain some line.

The "tip and roll" is always performed close to the end of a fight. It is a great way to get a fish to the boat quickly for a safe release.

54

The two-handed strip

SOME SALTWATER FISH REACT TO A FLY THAT IS
stripped as fast as possible. Tuna, barracudas, roosterfish, amberjacks,
and yellowtail are good examples. These guys prefer a fly that moves
like a racing car. If the fly isn't imitating a fleeting baitfish, and if it
suddenly stops or even pauses, these fish will turn and swim away.

Use a two-handed strip to imitate fast-moving bait.

The two-handed strip is the perfect retrieve for these situations. This retrieve enables the fly to be stripped through the water without breaks or pauses, as happens with the conventional one-handed strip. The drawback to using this retrieve is that you have to place the rod under your arm, which makes it almost impossible to lift the rod tip for a strike. Instead, you have to use a strip-strike.

For a successful two-handed strip, do the following:

1. After the cast, place the rod under one of your arms.
2. Point the rod tip down, keeping the tip in the water at all times.
3. Begin the strip by pulling the fly line with your hand at the first stripping guide.
4. Repeat this with the other hand.
5. There should be a continual motion, changing hands with each strip. Vary the speed of the fly as you strip it through the water.
6. Strip the fly all the way to the boat and repeat; if you feel a hit, give your line a solid strip-strike.

This is a great technique for blue water as well as nearshore fly fishing.

55

Warm-up stretch

YOU MAY NOT CONSIDER SALTWATER FLY FISHING a physical sport, but be advised that it's more physically demanding than fighting a rainbow or brown trout on the Henry's Fork.

The long and sandy stroll . . .

Saltwater gamefish are broad-shouldered fish that can have you cry-ing "uncle" if you are out of shape. Just ask the guy who has spent a day on the ocean battling a yellowfin tuna on a twelve-weight fly rod, or the guy who has spent an afternoon walking five miles in ankle-deep beach sand searching for the elusive roosterfish.

Just as athletes warm up before practice and competition, it can really make a difference if you stretch your arms, legs, and back before making your first cast. This rule is especially important to the middle-aged fly fisherman whose only physical activity is changing TV channels. Be smart . . . warm up!

PART

5

The Flies

56

Organize your fly box

AN ORGANIZED FLY BOX NOT ONLY REFLECTS ITS
owner's character, but also simplifies the process of selecting flies.
The well-organized box will allow you to select the correct fly
quickly in the heat of the moment, such as during a striper feeding
frenzy, thus giving you more time casting and less time rummaging
through piles of mixed feathers.

When stocking your fly box for bluewater fishing, make sure
to include baitfish patterns, crab and shrimp patterns, and poppers.
Most saltwater fish feed on some types of baitfish, so a selection
of flies in various colors and sizes will be an asset when trying to
match the baitfish in the place you are fishing. Divide your box
into two sections. Place the bigger flies on one side of the box, the
smaller crab and shrimp patterns on the other side. Coordinate and
organize all flies according to sizes and colors.

57

Choosing the correct baitfish fly

PICKING THE CORRECT FLIES IS ONE OF THE KEYS TO catching fish. This can be a daunting task for the beginning angler, as most tackle shop fly bins are filled with huge numbers of flies in all shapes, sizes, and colors. Here are some basic guidelines.

Baitfish Patterns

I believe that a sparsely dressed baitfish pattern is preferable to a bulked-up, flashy fly because it looks more natural. I've also found

Sometimes less is more.

that gamefish are far less selective when presented with a sparsely dressed fly. The fly is only a hint of what the fish is feeding on, and it often elicits a reflexive striking action. When gamefish do strike, they usually zero in on the fly's oversized eye, which closely resembles the large eyes of baitfish such as sardines, pilchards, and anchovies. For them, focusing on that eye results in fewer lost meals.

Color

Natural colors work best. Olive greens, browns, tans, and whites are all great color combos for baitfish patterns. Also, carry a selection of blue-and-white, red-and-white, and chartreuse-and-white flies, for those times when a bit more flash is called for.

Size

Fly size depends on what type of fish you're pursuing. In most saltwater fly-fishing situations, you'll need baitfish patterns that range from a small anchovy pattern in size 6 to a large sardine or pilchard pattern in size 2/0. Remember, it's all about matching the size of the baitfish that fish are feeding on.

58

Foolproof weed guard

THE HEAVY COVER FOUND IN MANGROVES, ESTUAR-
ies, sloughs, and flats always poses problems for fly fishermen, as their
flies constantly snag on eelgrass, turtle grass, and other vegetation.
The key to catching fish in these areas is keeping your fly free of the
salad and swimming naturally.

To make a foolproof weed guard, start with a piece of heavy,
hard mono (forty- to sixty-pound) and make a U shape directly
behind the eye of the hook. The piece should be long enough to
touch the point of the hook when it is bent back. Tie the mono
onto the shank, making certain that the U shape is at a ninety-
degree angle from the top of the hook (pointing straight down).
The mono will allow the fly to roll over the nasty stuff that flies
without weed guards continually snag.

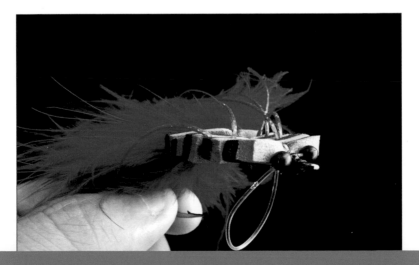

59

How to strip a Clouser Minnow

THE CLOUSER MINNOW IS ONE OF THE GREATEST flies ever invented for the saltwater fly angler. Bob Clouser initially created this fly to target smallmouth bass on the Susquehanna River in Pennsylvania. Since then it has been used to catch everything from surf perch to tarpon. The Clouser Minnow is, quite simply, a must-have fly in everyone's saltwater fly box.

All saltwater gamefish are predators to some degree. Bonefish root around the bottom looking for shrimp and crabs. Bonito pursue wandering mackerel, while tuna chase down and buzz-saw through schools of bait. All of them pick off injured and helpless baitfish as they fall away from the main school.

Because of its unique look, the Clouser Minnow is able to imitate a baitfish in any of these situations. For rooting fish, it can be stripped like a fleeing crab with short jerks of the line, making it hop and skitter across the bottom. Cast into a feeding frenzy of tuna, it's deadly when stripped quickly, allowed to fall for a few seconds, then stripped again, thus imitating a hurt or scared baitfish.

When stripping a Clouser, keep the rod tip on the water at all times. This will ensure a positive hook-set when the fly is taken by a gamefish.

60

Night fishing for snook: Best fly

FLY FISHING AFTER DARK IS SOMETHING ALL FLY FISH-
ers should experience—it's a real trip! The sounds, smells, and feel
are wonderfully exciting and exhilarating. Add some snook to this
mix and you have the makings of a memorable evening.

Snook are night feeders, and are particularly aggressive when
hiding in the shadows of illuminated piers, dock pilings, or man-
grove-covered banks. When a baitfish swims into the well-lit area, it
will become disoriented by the lights. This is when the snook will
pounce, grab its meal, then quickly swim back to the darker waters,
where it devours its prey.

Snook can be caught in these situations, but only if presented the proper fly. For my money, that fly would have to be a Black Marabou Toad, which has a long, flowing, rabbit fur tail. Cast it into the dark near a lighted pier, then retrieve it into the lighted area with quick, erratic strips. This motion, which resembles the darting and jumping of a confused baitfish, drives snook absolutely crazy.

Catching Fish

Barbed or barbless?

MANY FLY ANGLERS ARE ADVOCATES OF CATCH-AND-release angling. To this end, a barbless hook is easier to remove from a fish's mouth, thus enabling the angler to release it quickly.

A side benefit of the barbless hook is that it is far more effective at penetrating the fish's mouth than the traditional barbed hook. This is especially true with species that have super hard mouths, such as tarpon.

Unlike barbed hooks, barbless hooks are also more easily extracted from the backs of heads, ears, and other parts of the human anatomy.

Give the fish a break; de-barb your hook!

62

Bite tippet for barracudas

WHEN FLY FISHING THE FLATS FOR BONEFISH, YOU'LL often spot barracudas swimming into casting range. "Berries" should be cast to! But because a steel bite tippet is not a piece of the standard leader for bonefish, the chances of hooking and successfully bringing in the barracuda are slim, as their razor-sharp teeth will make fast work of any mono or fluorocarbon tippet. Here's a quick fix:

1. Take a six-inch piece of thirty-pound, single-strand, stainless steel wire, then make a very tight loop on one end with a Haywire Twist. Tie another Haywire Twist to the fly, leaving a loop in the fly end of the leader.
2. When fishing, keep this pre-rigged leader somewhere within reach (on your belt, or in a chest pack).
3. Once you spot a barracuda, take the prerigged leader with fly and slip it onto the hook of the fly you're using for bonefish.
4. Twist the stainless steel loop onto the bend of the bonefish fly hook, leaving just enough play in the loop so the barracuda fly and leader move freely but cannot detach while casting.

This method can save the day when the bonefish are tough to catch but the barracudas are willing to eat.

How to avoid bloody knuckles

AT SOME POINT IN YOUR SALTWATER FLY-FISHING career, you're going to get bloody knuckles from your reel's handle. This will happen when a big gamefish boils away at top speed, causing the handle to spin violently and bash your knuckles in the process. And while some anglers may consider bloody knuckles to be a badge of honor, most of us consider it a painful reminder not to hold onto the reel handle while fighting a fish. So what do we do with the reel hand when we are engaged in a tough fish fight?

First, never, under any circumstances, wrap your fingers around the reel handle that spins as the fish runs; if your fingers happen to be in the way, the handle will pummel your knuckles.

A better option is to hold the reel handle between your thumb, index finger, and middle finger, so when the fish makes its run you can let go of the handle and allow the spool to spin freely.

Whatever you do, don't grab that handle!

The bonefish challenge

ONE OF THE MOST SOUGHT-AFTER SALTWATER gamefish, the bonefish is elusive, spooky, and fast, a real challenge to the fly fisherman. Ranging in size from two to five pounds in the Caribbean, to eight to ten pounds in Florida and Hawaii, it lives in some of the most beautiful tropical settings in the world.

To find bonefish, look for areas where the fish are mudding or tailing in the crystal-clear shallow water of sand flats or coral reefs. Locating the fish, however, doesn't automatically mean hookups, as bonefish are always on the move, constantly changing directions, darting to all points of the compass.

For tackle, a six- to nine-weight rod matched with a large-arbor reel packed with 150 yards of backing and a float-ing line will work best in most situations. Use a ten- to twelve-foot leader, and practice casting with it before you actually go out on the water, as accurate presentations are critical.

◀ Any size bonefish is a trophy.

Striped bass

BORN AND RAISED ON THE WEST COAST, I HAVE HAD the good fortune and the opportunity to fish striped bass on the Sacramento Delta. These expansive brackish-water wetlands, that resemble the Louisiana marshes, stretch from Sacramento west to San Francisco Bay and boast some of the best striper bass fly fishing in the nation. Differing from the East Coast striper experience where this prime game fish is fished from the shoreline or from a boat in open water, this California brethren is fished in brackish or fresh water in the late fall or early winter months. He's a great fly-rod fish, easily accessible from shore, boat, or kayak in the Sac's abundant and fertile waters.

The tackle is very similar to that used on the Eastern seaboard: seven- or nine-weight rods, slow-sinking, 200- or 300-grain sinking lines, and short leaders (six to seven feet).

The key to success on this fishery is finding the bait. There are huge populations of baitfish in the Sac Delta, and the stripers will begin shadowing bait fish into the Delta beginning in early fall and continuing through the early spring.

Be alert for any sign of birds, terns, or seagulls "pecking" the water, a good indication that stripers are pushing small bait fish just below the water's surface, against banks, sheltered coves, or dock pilings.

Once you have pinpointed surface disturbances, make a cast into the center of the commotion, allow your fly to sink, then quickly apply very aggressive, erratic strips that will give your fly the appearance of an injured baitfish. Once your line comes tight, hang on and prepare yourself for a very strong, fulfilling, and rewarding fight.

East-Coast Stripers

Though separated by 3,000 miles, the Eastern-Seaboard striper resembles his West Coast cousin in feistiness and willingness to hit a variety of flies including the Clouser Minnow and Lefty's Deceivers, two streamers flies favored off the Cape Cod Coast, where the Striper is found in the early fall during his migration south.

Not unlike the West Coaster, he is found in estuaries, flats, jetties, along the surf-line and offshore, and can be fished wading, or drifting in boat or skiff; One sure way of finding this primo-game fish in open water is to follow movement of gulls and terns circling and diving into balls of bait fish. This is the signal to break out the nine- to eleven-weight rod, a reel loaded with either a sinking-shooting head in 250 or 300 grams. Lengthy casts are not required, but accuracy is of the essence. Make your cast ahead of the fish, allow your fly to sink, then, with your rod tip pointed at the fish, retrieve your line in well-spaced strips. One caution: Do not lift your rod tip on the strike; with the rod tip still pointed in the fish's direction, pull straight back to set the hook, and hang on!

While we are at it, the Bluefish—a toothy critter not found on the West Coast—is also deserving of consideration when affording space to the striper. Although at times a very elusive fish, when a school is found working a school of baitfish, you will find this guy more than willing to wrap his choppers around streamer and popper patterns; snookering one on the water's surface is an awesome fly-fishing experience. Because of the fish's razor-sharp incisors, make certain that you employ not only a good nine-weight rod but also, for good-measure, a light, single-strand wire leader. It's true that wire can spook this fish, but this fish is able to chew through mono with the precision of a cross-cut saw ripping through a two-by-four.

66

Chumming for makos

FOUND ON BOTH THE ATLANTIC AND PACIFIC COASTS, the mako shark is one of saltwater fly fishing's outstanding yet unappreciated gamefish. Hook one in the eighty- to 150-pound range, and you'll find yourself in a battle that will test all of your fish-fighting skills.

First things first. You're going to need a boat to get into this game. Ideally, you want a boat that's over eighteen feet, one that can handle fairly choppy seas. Most center consoles will do; however, a skiff with a beam of eight feet or wider and a not-too-deep V-hull will settle in the water better and reduce pitch and roll, making for a much more stable casting platform.

A chum line is the most effective way of attracting makos to within sight-casting distance of your boat. Chumming attracts larger makos, and will place you in the position of being able to pick and choose which fish you cast to.

To make a chum bag, first go to your local dock or fish market and try to find boats giving away belly sections or fresh carcasses of tuna, bluefish, or bonito. (Store-bought chum will suffice, if you can't find fresh.) Fill a burlap sack or store-bought chum bag, place it in a milk crate or five-gallon bucket and allow it to hang over the side. Once that chum slick begins to spread, it won't take long before any sharks in the area start to show up. One piece of advice: Less is more when chumming. You don't need much—no matter how small the slick, a shark can smell it from miles away.

Be patient when chumming. I will generally wait at least an hour and a half before moving to another spot. Once makos do find your slick and get into it, however, you can usually count on them sticking around for most of the fishing day. Drifting allows you to cover more water, and in the process attract more makos to your boat.

Use a stick to smash the carcasses and spread the fishy goodness.

67

California corbina from the beach

PERHAPS ONE OF THE MOST SKITTISH OF ALL THE West Coast gamefish, the California corbina is a ghostly apparition that glides through the shallow waters of flats and estuaries, or off beaches, in the late spring and throughout the summer. This fish is extremely wary, and it's rare to find him within casting range.

There is, however, one well-founded method of approaching corbina without spooking them. During early morning hours, when the light is softer and before the masses have hit the beach, look for corbina in the shallow waters of the tidal flats. This is a time of day when the fish feels more secure cruising into the shallow water to feed on mole crabs, bean clams, and small baitfish inside the surf line.

Before casting your first fly of the morning, stand back and spend a few minutes scanning the surf's whitewater, sandbars, and tidal flats, looking for the telltale signs that spell corbina. In particular, look for the backs of corbina as they work these areas, searching for food.

Once you have located some corbina, quietly move yourself to a point that gives you sight advantage on the shoreline, making certain that you don't step into the water. Corbina are sensitive to even the slightest noise in the surf zone, so wading into the surf can send them scurrying into deeper water. Cast from the beach, perhaps even from dry sand.

When making your casts, keep your body and rod in low profile so as not to alarm the fish; too much exposed body or an
overextended arm movement when casting will leave you staring
into empty tidewater. Everything connected with corbina fishing demands stealth. If they are not disturbed and are focused on
crab beds, corbina will often move so close that you can practically
touch them with your rod tip.

Cast at least twenty feet in front of the fish, making sure that the
fly doesn't hit the water too hard. Let it sink, then wait. Don't move
the fly! If the corbina is interested, it will hit your offering without
hesitation. Once hooked, it will scurry toward the safety of the surf
zone at speeds that rival those of the bonefish and permit, so hang
on!

A simple mole crab pattern will attract feeding corbina on the flats.

68

How to find fish in blue water

FINDING FISH IN BLUE WATER MAY SEEM TO BE A daunting task. The ocean is huge, and big gamefish such as tuna, dorado, sharks, and marlin can cover great distances in a matter of

hours. But with good eyes and a little common sense, you can indeed find these fish in open blue water.

The first clue to locating fish in open blue water is bird activity: working terns, gulls, and pelicans. Locate the circling and diving birds, and you'll find fish nearby. If you see birds floating on the water, you should fish the area anyway, as a raft of birds may indicate that baitfish and gamefish are in the area, just not actively feeding at that moment.

Once the birds and bait are located, look for gamefish agitating the water's surface in pursuit of baitfish. The gamefish will push the baitfish up from the depths, forcing the prey to explode out of the water, an activity easily spotted at long distances. When this happens, the birds will also be going crazy, diving into the melee to pick off baitfish at the surface.

If you don't see any birds. look for structure such as floating kelp paddies or weed lines. Baitfish like to congregate underneath these structures for shelter, and where there are baitfish . . . there are gamefish! Pull up next to these floating structures and cast a fly out along the edge. Make a few strips and see if anyone is home. Sometimes you can even see the fish stacked up underneath the structure.

◀ You may find other locals searching the kelp for fish.

69

How to fly-fish pier pilings

PIER PILINGS ATTRACT A VARIETY OF SALTWATER gamefish, including snook, spotted bay bass, and croakers, as they provide perfect cover from which these predators can ambush bait-

Pilings provide perfect cover for an ambush.

fish attracted by all the currents and eddies. Fishing pilings requires some specialized tactics, however.

The first order of business is to determine which side of the piling is the leeward side (the side sheltered from the blowing wind). Position yourself upwind from the leeward side, preferably during high and low tides, so that you are casting down toward the pilings, allowing the current to take your fly as close as possible to the structure. Drift the fly through the pilings if possible. You may hang up and lose a few flies to the pilings at first, but once you get the hang of it, you'll catch more fish if you can get your flies right into the middle of the structure.

Once the fly is in the zone, make two or three strips, then allow it to drift back into the pilings. Fish will often strike the fly as it dead-drifts back toward the structure. If your first four or five casts produce zilch, move to the next piling. Once you've caught a fish, continue to fish that piling until the action slows or stops, then move on.

70

How to catch redfish

CATCHING A REDFISH ON THE FLY IS ONE OF SALTWATER
fly fishing's greatest experiences. Not only are redfish willing to take
a variety of flies and poppers, they also have a tendency to feed in
very shallow water, making them the perfect saltwater fish for sight-
casting. There is something special about casting to a redfish tailing

Redfish weigh from four to forty pounds, but all feed the same way.

along a grassy marsh bank, then watching the fly disappear into its mouth and the line come tight.

The redfish game is simple. All you need is a nine-foot, seven- or eight-weight rod matched with a floating line and a fly reel that can carry 150 yards of backing. Use a standard nine-foot leader with a fifteen- to twenty-pound test leader. If you're fishing for tailing reds, a crab pattern or spoon fly will do the job. A good bet when surface fishing along mangroves or grassy banks is a popper that creates surface noise and a highly visible wake.

In your search for areas where redfish are feeding, give special attention to oyster beds, mangrove shorelines, and shallow flats, where more often than not you'll spot redfish rooting around and kicking up bottom mud in their search for crustaceans and other food. When redfish are focused on feeding, it's possible to move in very close to them, making long casts unnecessary.

Once you've spotted the fish, cast your fly close to its head, make a one-handed steady strip of your line, and get ready for a strike.

71

Taking the leopard shark

FROM EARLY SPRING THROUGH MIDSUMMER, LEOP-
ard sharks can be observed traveling in large schools along Southern
California's beaches. The leopard, or "leo," is a fairly docile critter,

A leopard shark will run you up and down the beach for forty minutes.

spending its time feeding on crabs and baitfish in the shallow estuaries and bays. It's one of the strongest fighting species you can catch while fishing from the beach. It's also one of the largest, with some fish weighing fifty pounds and more.

The preferred fly tackle for the leopard is an eight-weight rod matched with a reel holding a 200-grain shooting head, and a five-foot, twenty- to twenty-five-pound monofilament leader, topped off with a Crease Fly.

When stripped and paused, the Crease Fly will suspend just off the bottom, making it a tempting target for any leopards in the area. Once a leopard decides to strike, it will do so without hesitation, making for an exciting hookup and fight. Be cautioned that what may appear to be a good strike may be only a reaction strike, so false hooking is not uncommon.

72

Bonito and False Alabacore (Little Tunny)

BONITO AND FALSE ALBACORE ARE FAVORITES WITH saltwater fly fishermen. What bonito and false "albies" lack in size (a 12-pound fish is considered a trophy), these speedsters more than make up for by providing the fly angler fast-action, knuckle–

The offshore bonito bite in spring can deliver some of the largest fish of the season.

bruising runs, whether fishing offshore in a kayak, in a skiff plying the bay and inlet waters, or fishing off the jetties.

Fly anglers can look forward to year-round action on bonito on bays and near shore waters. The West Coast has two runs of bonito each year, one in the spring and another in the fall, the spring-run generally producing schools of larger fish that tend to prowl in schools searching for anchovies and sardines. Though smaller than their spring-run relations, the fall-run fish provide fly fishermen plenty of action, especially in the bays and off the jetties.

False albacore are a wonderful fly rod fish and have, over the past several years, become a highly sought after game fish for the salt-water fly-rodder. Beginning in September and peaking in November, these "speeding bullets" can be caught from New England to the Florida Keys. The "albies" feed the same as bonito, cruising in schools and looking for schools of anchovies to feast on. Fly fishing for "little tunny," as they are called, is some of the most exciting fly fishing found on either coast.

A seven- to nine-weight rod, matched with a solid, large arbor reel that can store a 250-grain shooting head and 150 yards of backing, will cover any situation, offshore, bay, inlet, or jetty.

A good selection of baitfish patterns should include the "Clouser Minnow," "Lefty's Deceiver," and "poppers" in sizes six to 1/0. I have known fly fishermen who have taken the bonito on weighted "Woolly Buggers," a fly normally associated with freshwater fishing. When fly fishing never forget the adage, "Necessity is the mother of invention."

Both bonito and false albacore are often very selective in what they take; therefore, a smaller, more scantily-dressed fly can often produce more fish than does the larger, heavily-dressed fly. Toting a few smaller, scantily-dressed flies is a good idea.

When using a popper, especially when fishing from jetties or around breakwater rocks, I like to use a popper as a "splash-attractor" with the fly, usually a "deceiver," as a "trailer."

73

Poppers for calico bass

IF YOU HAVE EVER FISHED FOR LARGEMOUTH BASS, you know how exciting it is to watch a hungry bass explode on a properly placed popper cast along a weed line. Well, advance your excitement meter about one hundred clicks, and you have popper fishing for West Coast calico bass. These saltwater cousins of the largemouth bass live in the dense kelp forests along the Southern California coast, lurking in pockets and ambushing prey at every opportunity. They feed in small packs, and when one is hooked, four or five other calicos usually follow their kin to the boat.

These fish readily take to poppers plopped into a kelp paddy's pockets. There are other methods of catching these gamefish, but nothing matches the adrenaline rush of watching your brightly colored bucktail popper disappear into a swirl of salt water, then having this hard-fighting fish on the end of your fly line. It's something every fly fisher should experience.

During their March-through-June spawning period, calicos surface and congregate in large schools along the coastal kelp beds, a prime time to grab the fly rod and, using a kayak, stand-up paddleboard (SUP), or small skiff, venture offshore into the far reaches of the paddies and cast large poppers into the breaks in the kelp. Sometimes the strike is so violent that the calico, while trying to engulf the lure, will knock the popper completely out of the water. Once hooked, he will usually head deep into the kelp forest, winding your line around the stalks as he descends.

This saltwater equivalent of a largemouth bass uses similar ambush techniques in the kelp.

Keep your eyes peeled for gulls hovering over the kelp beds, a sure sign that something is about to happen. When the birds begin descending to the water in ever-tightening circles, get a move on it, as a feeding frenzy is about to begin.

A fast-action, nine-foot, nine- or ten-weight rod will work well for this fly fishing. Use an intermediate fly line and a straight, five- to six-foot length of fifteen- to twenty-pound monofilament leader. As for flies, the bigger and noisier, the better.

74

How to safely release a shark

SHARKS ARE WONDERFUL FLY ROD GAMEFISH THAT readily take flies and always provide outstanding sight-casting opportunities, be they on the flats or in the blue water.

Once you have hooked, played, and brought the shark to the boat, the biggest challenge is releasing it, no easy task in light of the fish's size and unpredictable nature. Make a wrong move and it can prove disastrous.

The safest method of releasing a shark is through the use of a long-handled release stick, an instrument with an open-ended steel attachment on its business end.

Once a shark is brought to the boat, place this release tool in the fish's mouth, keeping tension on the line with the leader hand. Slide the stick into the hook gap and, applying light pressure, push the fly. The shark will release itself without harm to itself or to you. The job will be even easier if you use barbless hooks.

A long-handled release stick keeps sharp teeth ▶ at a safe distance.

Use smaller flies for tuna and catch more fish

TUNA, INCLUDING BONITO, ALBACORE, AND LITTLE tunny (false albacore) have exceptional eyesight, and can size up bait better than any other saltwater fish. If you are attempting to pass off any old pattern rather than matching the size of the bait being eaten, you are not going to enjoy much success.

The tuna will focus on one size of bait, and if your fly is even a tad larger than the bait, you will get refusal after refusal—which means it's time to switch to smaller flies.

If you're getting refusals even though you are stripping the fly fast enough, and you find the tuna following but not taking, scale down the size of the fly you are using, making certain it is smaller than the bait; if you are experiencing difficulty determining exactly what the fish are feeding on, tie on the smallest fly you have. I have on occasion used bonefish flies (sizes 4 to 6) for tuna, finding that the smaller flies work well when all else fails. Just make certain the hooks are extra strong. The last thing you want is hook failure once you've latched onto a monster.

Presenting a smaller baitfish pattern often results in more frequent bites. ▶

How to find fish in the surf zone

THE SURF ZONE IS A GREAT PLACE TO START SALTWA-
ter fly fishing, whether you're targeting stripers on the East Coast or
corbina on the West Coast. This bewildering area of crashing surf,
rips, rock piles, and sandbars can be intimidating to the uninitiated.
Don't let it get to you! These two simple clues about surf zone
structure will help calm your doubts.

Extreme low tide is a good time to check out structure that is
normally underwater.

Rip Currents

Fish that live along beaches love structure, especially rip currents. These are small channels, usually twenty to thirty feet wide, created by waves washing on shore and then needing someplace to get back out to sea. These riverlike indentations run perpendicularly through the surf zone. Fish congregate on the edges or even within the rip to feed on baitfish, crabs, and shrimp. Rips can be very productive on both incoming and outgoing tides, and can be found along the edges of reef structures, alongside pier pilings, and randomly along sandy beaches.

Potholes

Where you find rip currents, you'll also find potholes, which are dark indentations located from a few feet to a few hundred feet from the shoreline. When you're observing a beach at low tide, try to remember the locations of potholes. Fish will stack up in them when the tide rises and covers them with water. They will, however, change location as the sand moves around.

77

Feeding a fly to a tarpon

WATCHING A TARPON TAKE A FLY AND TAKE OFF, planing, jumping, and twisting, is an exhilarating experience. To make it happen, you need to master the art of fly presentation.

First, no matter whether a tarpon approaches from left to right or right to left, never cast behind the fish, as this can spook him. Always place the fly ten to twenty feet beyond and above him at about a ninety-degree angle to his line of travel.

Allow the tarpon to swim to the fly, making certain not to move it until the fish has closed in; then, once the fish is positioned practically nose-to-nose with the fly, begin a slow, long, stripping retrieve. Think of it as teasing a cat with a toy mouse. Move the mouse too quickly and the cat loses interest; move it too slowly and it will not chase. Find the right speed and the cat will go for the mouse. In the same way, apply the right speed and tarpon will attack the fly. Strip it too fast, however, and you'll spook him.

Once a tarpon is focused on your fly, speed up the retrieve. Don't stop it! Keep it moving, and chances are he'll take it. When he does, give the fly a hard strip-strike. The tarpon's mouth is full of hard plates, and a timid strike won't allow the hook to penetrate. Drive that hook home, then hold on for the fight of your life!

There are few soft spots in the tarpon's mouth, so give a good hard strip-strike to set the hook.

78

Winter saltwater fly fishing

WINTER CAN BE THE BEST TIME OF YEAR TO CATCH saltwater fish on the fly. The beaches, flats, and bays are practically deserted in wintertime, as most fair-weather fishermen have retreated to their firesides. It's time for the serious fly flinger to put on his thermals, grab his fly rod, and head for the water.

Two of my favorite wintertime fish are the speckled trout (or spotted seatrout) and the black drum, both species that thrive in

Speckled trout will keep you busy all winter.

cool water. The speckled trout is a coastal fish found on shallow mud and sand flats from North Carolina to Texas. A fish that generally travels in large schools, it's capable of providing fast action on the fly, whether you're wading or fishing from a skiff, a kayak, or a larger boat.

One proven way to locate specks is to look for depressions, channels, holes, and cuts on or along the flats. Once you have located a school, cast into the middle with a floating or intermediate line, a nine-foot leader, and a baitfish pattern such as a weedless Bend Back.

The key to catching speckled trout in cold water is to retrieve the fly *slowly*, using short, jerky strips. The strike is often as light as an aunt's peck on the cheek, so keep a close watch on your fly.

My other favorite winter fish, the black drum, is found on the same types of flats as the speckled trout. Also called common drum, this gamefish can weigh from five to fifty pounds. Look for them near breakwaters, pier pilings, channels, estuaries, and marshes.

I remember catching my first black drum, also known as a "swamp donkey." It was a bitter-cold January day. I was fishing for redfish (red drum) in Louisiana and spied a large fish tailing next to the shoreline. At first I thought it was a big redfish, but as I got a closer look, I realized it was an enormous black drum. My guide suggested I cast, and try to drop my crab fly right on the fish's nose. As soon as the fly hit the water, the fish turned, inhaled the fly, and took off, making a run that took me deep into my backing. Once I got the fish under control and finally played it back to the boat, I realized that I had found a new favorite gamefish.

The black drum is a finicky eater, and does not strike quickly or with vigor—but once hooked, he's a handful. If you decide to brave the winter elements and try for him, go with a nine- or ten-weight rod, a floating weight-forward line, a nine-foot leader, and a pocketful of crab patterns (black drum love crustaceans).

PART

7

Mother
Nature

79

How deep is a fathom?

THIS MAY SOUND STRANGE, BUT THIS IS A QUESTION
I hear more than any other question when guiding in salt water:
How deep is a fathom?

The question may seem irrelevant; however, if you ever have to
read a nautical chart, you'll notice that most charts record depths
in fathoms, not feet.

Understanding how to read a chart can help you in navigating
a channel, finding a secret hot
spot, avoiding a sandbar, and,
most important, getting back
to the dock at the end of the
day.

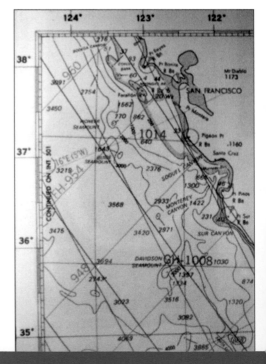

Here are some useful con-
versions for reading a nautical
chart.

1 fathom	= 6 feet
1 nautical mile	= 1.2 miles
1 knot	= 1.2 mph
1 meter	= 3.3 feet

80

Most productive tides: Rising and falling tides

I REMEMBER FISHING OFF THE BEACH WHEN I WAS A boy, and noticing that once the water along the beach began to churn, I began catching fish. It was as if someone had turned on a switch, causing the water to come alive with baitfish, bird life, and hookups. A few years later I figured out that the ocean turbulence and activity were the result of a changing tide.

Tides are very important to fishing success in both offshore and inshore waters, dictating where the fish will feed, and when they will feed. Being familiar with the tide's ebb and flow will improve your chances for success, no matter where you fish.

Marshes, Flats, and Beaches—Tides Transport Bait

I find the rising tide to be the optimum time to fish. Flood tides bring in new water filled with baitfish, shrimp, and other forage for gamefish to feast on.

Rising tide brings in an abundance of baitfish ▶ and crustaceans.

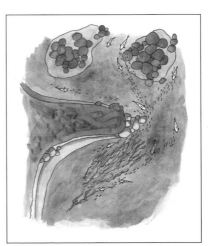

The gamefish will herd the bait into tight groups. Like the bad guys in a Western flick lying in wait for the good guys, the gamefish lie in wait to ambush the bait as it moves into nearshore areas, using the shoreline as a trap.

As the tide falls, the receding water pulls small, tasty creatures out of the rocks and marsh grass.

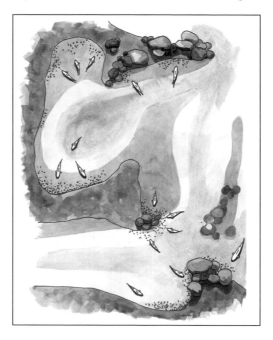

Falling tides that flush out marshes, estuaries, and flats can prove beneficial to the saltwater fly fisherman, as gamefish predictably will wait in deep channels and holes, and on sandbars for a seafood buffet being swept toward them.

Offshore—Tide-creating Currents

Fishing offshore tides is different from fishing nearshore tides. Instead of the flooding and draining effect that tides have on inland flats and marshes, offshore tides are more about the movement of water, or current. This water movement is generated by both tide and wind. And the greater the current, the better the fishing. How does this occur? As water moves over offshore structure, drop-offs, rock piles, and even floating kelp rafts, the currents push the bait into tight groups, making them easier prey for predatory gamefish.

Tides and Moon Phase

Tidal movements correspond with the moon phase, with the most extreme tides occurring during new and full moons. Fishing during these times is usually most productive. Keep in mind, however, that a full moon allows fish to feed all night. When the moon is full, fishing at dusk and dawn is often most productive.

Remember: The more tidal movement or current (water moving in, out, or in a certain direction), the better the fishing!

Full and new moons produce strong tidal movements, which concentrate the bait.

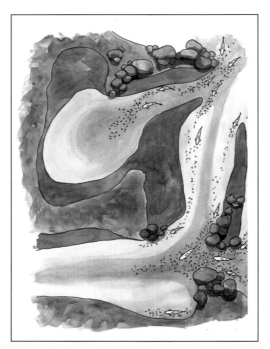

81

Stormy weather with dark clouds: Run for cover

CHANGING WEATHER CONDITIONS ARE PART OF fishing. One moment the sky will be blue and the sun will be shining. The next moment, ominous black clouds with lightning, off-the-chart winds, and torrential rains will take over the day. Luckily, today's anglers are able to access any number of weather-predicting sites that provide up-to-the-minute data that will help them decide whether to stay home or get out on the water.

Common sense should also dictate what you decide to do, no matter how hot the fishing might be. If you are on the water and notice a potential storm on the horizon, run for shelter if you are fishing a beach or flats. If you are on the ocean, aim your boat's bow toward safe harbor. Once the storm has passed, return to your fly fishing. Be safe, not sorry.

◄ If you see this . . .
run for cover!

82

What to do about glassy water

IT HAPPENS ALL THE TIME. YOU'RE OUT FISHING, AND the water is as slick as glass. You can see the fish, but at the same time, they can also see you. Not only that, but they can also detect your vibrations when you wade, pole your skiff, or try to move in close

A little texture on the water gives fish a sense of security and allows you to throw a fly without spooking them.

by using your outboard. How can you get within range of them for a cast?

The fish will become skittish is you get too close. Just when you're about to give up, however, a breeze picks up, the water assumes some texture, and all of a sudden the fish are turned on and you've got a feeding frenzy on your hands.

Anglers have different theories on why fish feed more aggressively when the breeze picks up. My thought is that choppy water gives fish a feeling of security, and they're less vulnerable when feeding.

The point is that when you're faced with glassy water conditions, with fish not in a feeding mood, don't give up. Wait a bit, and the minute the water develops a small chop, begin laying out line.

PART

8

The Traveling Saltwater Fly Fisherman

83

Fourteen essential items to pack for a saltwater fly-fishing trip

1. Pliers

Pliers have a number of functions. They make it easier to release fish, aid in pinching down hook barbs, cut wire or heavy monofilament, and open bottled beverages to quench your thirst on a hot day.

2. Tippet Material

Always carry enough monofilament or fluorocarbon to create leaders to meet your needs. Three spools of tippet material should suffice for most situations: twenty-, thirty-, and forty-pound test.

3. Towel

Once fish slime is on your hands, this sticky and smelly gunk will foul everything within reach: your gear, your clothes, the ham-and-cheese sandwich that you brought for lunch. Always carry a good, absorbent towel, one that can get the gunk off your hands and that can be rinsed after every use.

4. Sunblock

Besides ruining a fly-fishing trip, sunburn can ruin your life. Today's market is glutted with every sort of sun-protection ointment, and many provide excellent protection from the sun's rays. Once you have applied sunblock (do it more than once a day), rinse you hands thoroughly, as many fish can smell the chemicals on your fly or line. To be extra safe, wear it in conjunction with sun-protective clothing . . . and a hat.

5. Raingear

Even if it's sunny and hot when you head out fishing, it might get cloudy and cold, or windy and rainy, before the day is over. Always take raingear whenever you go, just in case. It also pays to take along a large garbage bag to protect your gear.

The essentials

6. Super Glue

Nothing is more annoying (and painful) than a cut or cracked finger while saltwater fishing. Whether you're on a flat in Belize or sixty miles offshore, Super Glue will close the cut and stop the bleeding, letting you keep fishing until you are able to deal with the condition back at the dock. Super Glue can also come in handy when you need to repair broken rod tips.

7. Duct Tape

As one of my fishing buddies once stated, "Duct tape is like The Force . . . it has a light side and a dark side and it holds the universe together." Like Super Glue, duct tape can take care of your many needs, be it securing a fly reel onto a broken reel seat, taping rod cases together for the flight home from a far-off location, or applying around your stripping finger for protection from the line.

8. Antibacterial Gel

When you're catching and releasing fish, there are going to be times when your hands suffer small nicks and cuts from razor-sharp teeth and spiny fins. An easy way to avoid nasty infections is to carry a pocket-size container of antibacterial hand wash and apply it generously throughout the day.

9. Gloves

Don't try to release or handle any fish bare-handed. Many fish have teeth, spines, stingers, and gills that can pierce your skin and cause infections. Wear good fishing gloves for any fish-handling chores.

10. Handheld Scale

The BogaGrip (with built-in scale) or another type of handheld scale will provide an accurate weight on that saltwater fish of a lifetime. Such scales pack easily and are worth every penny.

11. Hook Sharpener

Dull hooks are responsible for many lost fish. Even though many hooks are laser- or machine-sharpened, most saltwater fly hooks are made of stainless steel. When fished in rough areas such as jetties, rocks, coral, and even sandy bottoms, hooks will dull over time, and require constant sharpening. A good sharpener should always be a part of your kit.

12. Handheld GPS

One of the worst fishing nightmares is becoming lost or disoriented on the ocean, on the flats, or in a marsh's maze. A global positioning system (GPS) unit can prevent such situations. Using a GPS unit, you can also mark areas where the fishing is red hot, letting you return to the exact spot whenever you choose. Most GPS units contain moon phase and tidal information, both keys to successful fishing.

13. Headwear

A wide-brimmed hat can protect your nose, ears, and the back of your neck from sunburn. Don't wear a baseball hat unless you don't have a choice, as they afford only minimal protection from the sun's rays.

14. Tackle Bag

When shopping for a traveling tackle bag, choose one that will hold all the gear needed on your trip. Ideally, the bag should be made of a tough material and have many heavy-duty interior and exterior pockets. If you're going to fill it up, or if you're going to spend a lot of time going through airports, get a duffel bag with wheels.

84

No black-soled shoes!

IF YOU EVER GET A CHANCE TO FISH WITH A BUDDY whose skiff has a light-colored deck, don't wear black-soled sneakers, sandals, or loafers. If you do, don't be surprised if he never invites you to go on another fishing trip. There is nothing more annoying to a boat owner than black skid marks ornamenting his pride and joy from bow to stern, and being left to scrub them all off by himself. Leave the black-soled footwear at home.

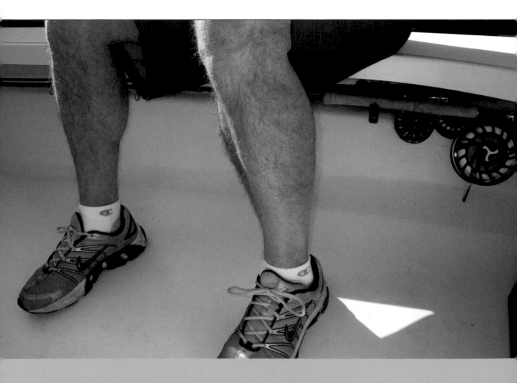

85

Pack light

MANY FLY FISHERMEN FESTOON THEIR VESTS WITH useless stuff: dull-bladed scissors, wool fly patches, and rust-encrusted hemostats. In addition, they cram their vest pockets full with fly

A waist pack is all you need when fishing the beach or flats.

boxes of every size, each pocket on the verge of popping its stitch-ing. And I would be remiss if I neglected to add the gigantic strip-ping baskets to my list of gear that serves no purpose other than to get in the angler's way. When fly fishing in salt water, go light.

Many places, such as beaches or flats, will force you to travel light—toting nonessential gear will wear you out over the course of a day. If you're going to be fishing in a skiff with a guide, ask him ahead of time what you need. In most cases, he'll have most of the gear anyway. Just bring your rods (two rods and reels will cover most situations) and a deck bag with necessities only. Leave the other stuff in your garage or tackle locker.

86

Learn from your guide

A GOOD GUIDE CAN PROVIDE YOU WITH A WEALTH of the information you need when fly fishing unfamiliar waters. His time spent on the water, logging hundreds of hours, studying the characteristics of different gamefish, and honing fly-fishing skills are almost guaranteed to make you a better angler. When you go to a different location and want to fish, hiring a guide is a worthwhile investment. Once you have enlisted his assistance, pay attention: Listen and learn! You might be a fly-fishing whiz on Montana's Beaverhead River, but you will find that saltwater fly fishing is entirely different from fly fishing in fresh water. Don't bend his ear with stories about your skills as a freshwater angler. You are there to learn from *him,* not vice versa.

Find a good guide and you may make a lifelong friend in the process.

87

Preserve your memories: Take quality photographs

THERE IS NOTHING BETTER THAN SEEING A BEAU-
tifully composed photograph of an angler with his saltwater trophy.
Choosing the correct lighting, background, and angle can enhance
any photo, and can make the difference between an average snap-
shot and something worth framing.

The memories a photograph can hold are priceless and something to be admired for years. Who doesn't want a photo of his hefty tarpon, caught on a fly in the Florida Keys?

There are now many affordable, easy-to-use, waterproof digital cameras on the market. Buy a good one; it will return your investment many times over. And learn how to use it *before* you take that one-week bonefishing trip to the Abacos.

When shooting, remember that good lighting is critical. Early mornings and late afternoons are the best times for taking photographs, as the light during these times of the day tends to accentuate the best colors. Bright sunlight in the middle of the day, on the other hand, is not ideal. It casts harsh shadows on the faces of anglers and on the fish. If you catch a good fish in the middle of the day and have to take photos in bright sunlight, shoot with the sun at your back and consider using a fill flash to illuminate your subject's face.

Be creative. Share the shot with your fish. Don't, for instance, just lift the fish out of the water and hold it up to the camera and smile. Perhaps a better shot would be to hold the fish halfway out of the water and shoot the photos from an angle, thus getting a well-composed picture of you and your trophy.

Always make the fish the focus of the photo. Whether your fish is the catch of a lifetime or your first catch of a given species, remember that the fish is the most important part of the photo.

Finally, taking a picture rather than turning your trophy over to a taxidermist allows you to release your fish unharmed to fight another day. Try fishing CPR . . . **C**atch, **P**hotograph, and **R**elease. Smile!

88

Preparation: The key to a successful fly-fishing trip

THERE IS NO SUBSTITUTE FOR WELL-THOUGHT-OUT preparation when it comes to taking a saltwater fly-fishing trip. But for one reason or another, many anglers don't take the time to plan things out ahead of time, an error that can result in not having the right gear or clothing, ineffective casting (from not practicing before the trip), poor fly selection (from not studying an area's gamefish ahead of time), not to mention all the extra cash you'll have to shell out to buy the right equipment once you get to your destination. Here are a few things to consider when planning for your first saltwater fly-fishing trip:

1. A week or so prior to your trip, spend a half hour each day, or as time allows, casting into the wind, practice that will prepare you for those unforgiving, blustery winds you will encounter when fishing the flats and offshore. Work on distance. Casts of forty to fifty feet with no more than two false casts are a must.

2. Research which flies you'll need for the waters you're going to fish. If you are going to fish with a guide, ask him what flies are appropriate, and whether your guide will be providing them for you. Too many anglers show up at their destination with flies that are better suited for catching bluegills or trout, not saltwater species. Do your homework!

3. Be in shape: Hit the gym. Get a physical. Many saltwater fishing destinations place extreme physical demands upon the angler, especially locations in the tropics, where sun and wind can sap your strength in a hurry. Get off the couch and go for a walk. Your body will thank you.

4. Pack your bags, then repack them to eliminate unnecessary items. Pack only those things that you will absolutely need:

Don't bring too much extra gear,
but make sure you don't forget any of the essentials.

tackle, clothes, toilet articles, medications if necessary. Above all, do not duplicate if it's not necessary.

5. If your trip is to a foreign country, study the culture, customs, and perhaps the language spoken by the natives. Having some background information on your destination can only help in the long run. Don't forget your passport—make sure it hasn't expired, and take a copy just in case.

Remember, if you are well prepared, you will have a much more enjoyable trip than if you were unprepared.

PART

9

Safety

89

Be prepared for a medical emergency

MANY SALTWATER FLY-FISHING DESTINATIONS ARE in beautiful but remote locations that have few or no medical services. If you get sick or hurt, you could be in trouble.

Before you leave for a trip, research the medical services that are available at your destination, and plan accordingly. Also make sure to pack a comprehensive first-aid kit, complete with antibiotics, pain relievers, bandages (and tape), diarrhea medicine, and insect repellent.

To ensure your safe return home in case of serious sickness or injury, by all means purchase evacuation travel insurance.

Bug repellent is a must in most saltwater destinations.

90

How to remove a hook painlessly

WITH WINDY CONDITIONS AND EVER-CHANGING casting directions, sooner or later you, your fishing partner, or your guide is going to get hooked by a fly. When it happens, hopefully it will be with a barbless hook, which is much easier to extricate from your arm, leg, back, or worse, your ear, than a barbed hook. Here's how to remove a hook painlessly and quickly:

1. Make a loop on the end of a piece of heavy monofilament, and place the loop around the embedded hook's gap.
2. Holding the tag ends of the mono loop, press down on the hook's eye.
3. A quick pull will free the hook from the victim's flesh.

After the hook is removed, thoroughly cleanse the wound. See a doctor if needed.

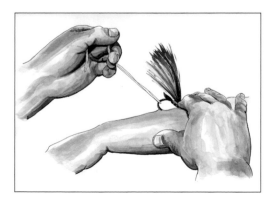

91

How to prevent seasickness

THERE IS NO WORSE FEELING THAN BEING ON THE ocean and having your innards suddenly go into nauseous convulsions. You're the victim of a scourge that has plagued humankind since we first hoisted a sail on the ocean. Its common name is seasickness, though those who have suffered from it may also call it "sea death," as many folks would rather be thrown to the sharks to put them out of their misery. It isn't fun.

Without getting into the medical reasons behind seasickness, there are a couple of things you can do to help avert having it happen to you.

First, watch what you eat the night before you go fishing. Eat light. A double helping of lasagna with some garlic bread and red wine on the side is going to sit in your stomach all night, and still be there the next morning.

If you eat light, yet still suspect that you're going to feel ill on the water, consider taking an over-the-counter medicine such as Dramamine or Bonine before you go out. Ear patches, wrist bands, and other medications can also be obtained, though in most cases you'll need a prescription from your doctor.

What has worked for many of my clients over the years is a teaspoon of pickled ginger, the kind you can get at your local sushi restaurant or Asian market. For some reason, this remedy works almost all the time. If you're on the water and start to get an upset stomach, eat a teaspoon of ginger—you'll be amazed at the results.

One old-timer's method for curing seasickness is to look at the horizon or a landmark and avoid looking down, a move that usually triggers the nausea.

Another trick, used by one of my older fishing buddies, is to never go out on the ocean without a box of Saltine crackers. Eating a few crackers always worked for him.

If all else fails, start the boat and motor into the wind. A breeze on your face will help you feel better.

Check the conditions before you head out.

92

Learn how to run a skiff

WE TALK SO MUCH ABOUT HOW TO PICK THE RIGHT flies, cast into the wind, and fight fish, but we rarely cover the importance of being able to operate a skiff if called upon to do so.

It's simple. If you're on the water in a boat or skiff, miles offshore or somewhere on the flats, and your guide, captain, or fishing buddy is for some reason unable to run the skiff—perhaps due to illness or injury—it's critical that you know how to run the craft back to shore and safety. The chances are slim that this will actually happen, but you never know. It happened to me once, and I'll forever be thankful that I knew how to operate a boat.

One painless way to learn the basics of running a boat is to enroll in a boating and water safety class.

When heading out for a day on the water, make a point of familiarizing yourself with the skiff's or boat's power unit. How does the motor start—with a key-controlled electric starter, or with a manual pull cord?

Does the boat or skiff have a center console with steering wheel, or is the motor moved by a tiller? Is there a kill switch that will deactivate the motor if the switch is detached from the key?

Where is the boat's GPS and navigation unit? Is it set to track back to the boat's launching point? Does the craft have a VHF radio? How is it operated and, in an emergency, how do you contact the Coast Guard?

And last, but hardly least: Where are the personal flotation devices and first-aid kit?

Familiarize yourself with all these aspects of boat operation, and you'll be able to return the boat and its passengers to safety if something happens to the boat's operator.

Knowing how to operate a skiff can be useful in an emergency situation.

93

Sun protection

I KNOW IT LOOKS GREAT TO HAVE A TAN, BUT IN truth, that tan can eventually turn into skin cancer—and if you get melanoma, it can kill you. Here are some ways to keep those rays off your skin.

Stay covered up to avoid the sun's harmful rays.

Sunblock

The recommended strength for sunblock varies. Some doctors say SPF 15 is adequate; many dermatologists say you should use nothing less then SPF 30. Whatever strength you decide to use, be smart and, during your day on the water and in the sun, take the time to reapply sunblock frequently, especially to your nose, ears, hands, and face—the parts of the body that take the brunt of the sun's rays. After application, be sure to clean your hands thoroughly so you don't get any sunblock on your fly or line. Gamefish can detect the odor and may spook.

Clothing

The best way to protect your skin is to completely cover your body with proven protective clothing. Most new outdoor wear is not only comfortable and functional, but has an SPF rating of 30-plus, which provides you with extra protection. These outfits come in an assortment of colors and styles for even the most fashion-conscious saltwater fly rodder.

Headgear

A hat is one of the most basic elements of sun protection. There is such a huge variety of hats available that it's largely a matter of preference. Some folks prefer the standard baseball cap, which provides moderate protection. Watch out for mesh trucker's caps, however, as the sun will penetrate right through the mesh. A wide-brimmed hat that covers your ears as well as your head and neck is better for overall protection. Then there's the balaclava, which is currently very popular and can be worn completely over the face, on the neck, or merely on the head. Several versions are available, and can be adapted to hot, warm, or cold conditions.

PART
10

Tackle Care

94

The best way to clean fly line

KEEPING YOUR FLY LINE CLEAN IS AS IMPORTANT as keeping rust off your hooks. Fly lines are exposed to all sorts of harmful things over the course of a fishing day or season. Heat, dirty salt water, sunscreen, and bug repellent can all harm your fly line. All will shorten your line's life if not gotten rid of.

Regularly cleaning your fly line will help increase the distance of your casts and extend the life of your line.

To clean a fly line, basic dish soap and warm water work about as well as anything. Take the line and strip it off into a bucket containing dish soap and warm water. Allow the line to soak in the bucket for two or three minutes, then rinse it with fresh water. Next, take a clean cloth or sponge and wipe off the entire line before winding it back onto your reel. Your cleaning cloth will show you how much dirt was on the line.

To add a little extra slickness to your line, wipe it with a coating of silicone or fly line dressing after cleansing—this can add distance to your casts.

To get the most out of your fly line, give it a good bath after every couple of trips in salt water.

95

Keep your grip dry

WHEN RINSING OFF YOUR FLY ROD AFTER FISHING, be careful not to soak the cork grip. If the cork handle becomes waterlogged, the glue securing it to the rod will be compromised, and the grip could separate from the rod. When this happens, your casting will suffer, as the rod won't react the way it should. You'll be unable to properly tighten your reel to the reel seat, and sooner or later you're going to have a repair job on your hands.

Once you return from a trip, thoroughly rinse off all your gear, but don't put the rod the back in its case right away. Let it air dry completely before storing.

After a freshwater rinse, dry and store your gear.

96

Care of polarized lenses

POLARIZED EYEWEAR SHOULD BE AN INTEGRAL part of your fishing arsenal. Finding a pair of polarized glasses that you like will take time and money, but the investment will be well worth it, as high-quality eyewear will save your eyes from the blistering sun. It will also cut the glare on the water, allowing you to spy fish that you wouldn't otherwise be able to see.

To get the most out of your polarized sunglasses, it's important to clean them correctly. Fresh water and either a chamois or camera lens cloth will do the job quite well. Make sure that the cloth you use is clean and stays that way by storing it in a dry, secure container, such as a locking plastic bag. Whatever you do, don't wipe your eyewear with toilet paper, paper towels, or your shirt. Toilet paper and paper towels are made from wood products and will scratch your glasses. Your shirt will pick up salt particles, dirt, and grime, which can also scratch and ruin your lenses.

I would also advise to stay away from commercially produced glass and lens cleaners. Although they work well for some glasses, such cleaners contain chemicals that will eventually remove your glass's polarizing film. The same can also be said for sunscreens.

Finally, consider lightly oiling the metal hinges on your glasses to prevent saltwater corrosion.

Protect your eyewear investment by giving it the same attention and care you give to your rods, reels, and other equipment.

Use fresh water when cleaning polarized lenses.

97

Rinsing your fly reel

SALT WATER IS CORROSIVE AND A REAL THREAT TO
your equipment, especially your fly reel, which is perhaps the most
vulnerable of all your gear. Your reel not only takes a beating from

Salt water will ruin even the best reel.
A quick rinse makes a big difference.

fighting fish, but it also gets tossed around on boats and on sandy beaches, and suffers the occasional dunk in salt water or roll in the sand. In light of these threats, it pays to pamper your reel. Wash it after every trip to the salt.

The correct way to remove saltwater residue from your reel is to take a hose with a spray nozzle and adjust it to the fine-mist setting. Spray your reel lightly without forcing water into its working parts. When finished, dry the reel with a clean rag or car chamois. It's that simple. At the end of the season, give it a thorough washing by taking it apart, rinsing and drying every part, then applying oil or grease to all moving parts. I also advocate returning your reel to the manufacturer for periodic tune-ups. Treat your reel as well as you treat your car (or better). You've got a lot riding on that one piece of equipment.

98

How to keep hooks from rusting

THERE IS NOTHING MORE ANNOYING THAN REACH-
ing into your fly box and pulling out a fly with a rusty hook. Salt
water will rust and corrode a hook overnight, and if you think that
stainless steel hooks are not affected by salt water, guess again.

There are a couple of ways to keep rust from ruining your
favorite patterns. One way is to spray your flies with a light mist of
fresh water at the end of each day, then let them air dry thoroughly.

Don't waste a good box of flies. Give them a rinse!

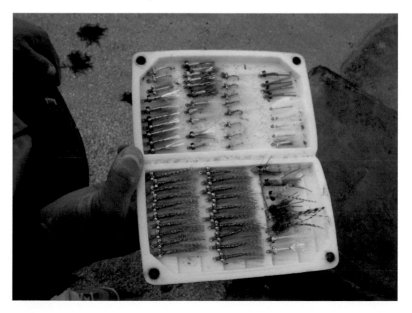

Whatever you do, don't use a hair dryer, unless you want to end up with a gooey ball of feathers.

Mild dish soap also works well. Put a drop in a container with fresh water, drop your flies in, replace the lid, and give it a good shake. Next, pour out the water and rinse the flies with more fresh water. Finally, set them out to air dry.

You may also want to hit your flies with a little WD-40 at the end of your trip. This will add a protective coating to your hooks, one that will keep rust at bay. Just be careful not to saturate them, or your flies will become gummy with oil.

PART

11

On the Water

99

Don't crowd your neighbor

ENCROACHING ON SOMEONE'S SPACE CAN MAKE people uncomfortable and can get downright ugly. Have you ever had another fisherman cast over your line? Or perhaps you're running a chum line and another boat cuts right through the middle of it? How about having another boat crowd you while you're trying to cast to surface-feeding fish? Or, what if another angler crowds you when you're fishing a quiet stretch of beach?

Fishing shoulder to shoulder is annoying and can be dangerous.

These are all prime examples of one angler invading another angler's space. Ultimately, they're cases of bad manners. And sadly, this type of behavior happens all too often.

Unless you wish to be branded a lowlife (or worse), avoid confrontations with fellow anglers by observing good on-the-water manners. When sharing a stretch of beach, it is always a good practice to allow at least one hundred yards between you and other shore anglers. If someone is fishing a particular area, stay clear— if you must pass him, walk quietly around him, allowing enough room for him to continue making his backcasts. And never walk up to him and break his concentration by blurting, "How's the fishing?"

Treat other anglers the way you'd like them to treat you, and we'll all be better off.

100

Maximize your time
on the water

OVER THE YEARS, I'VE RUN INTO ANGLERS WHO think that having high-end rods, reels, huge fly selections, and the latest waders will ensure them a high degree of success. What they did not take into account was how much work, practice, and dedication it takes to be a successful saltwater fly angler. They assumed that a few weeks of practicing the double haul was enough to make them skilled enough to catch lots of fish.

Practice is fine, but the truth of the matter is that nothing can match spending time on the water. It doesn't matter whether you're casting flies to surf perch on a local beach or fishing offshore for tuna—time spent fishing will help you hone your skills. Catching fish is of secondary importance.

The key is to try to learn something each time you hit the water. If the bonefishing is tough on the flats, practice casting into the wind. If no makos are showing up in your chum slick, practice tying the Bimini Twist. If there are no stripers along the beach, try to figure out the best tides and areas to fish.

Sight casting to a rolling tarpon in Belize

PART

12

Good Reads

101

Read a good book

This book would not be complete without giving you a reading list to get you through the slow days. Here are some of my favorites.

Adams, Aaron J. *Fisherman's Coast: An Angler's Guide to Marine Warm-Water Gamefish and Their Habitats* (Stackpole Books, 2003)

Adams, Aaron J. *Fly Fisherman's Guide to Saltwater Prey* (Stackpole Books, 2008)

Blanton, Dan. *Fly-Fishing California's Great Waters* (Frank Amato Publications, 2003)

Combs, Trey. *Bluewater Fly Fishing* (Lyons and Burford, 1995)

Curcione, Nick. *Baja on the Fly* (Frank Amato Publications, 1997)

Curcione, Nick. *The Orvis Guide to Saltwater Fly Fishing* (The Lyons Press, 1993)

Curcione, Nick. *Tug-O-War: A Fly-Fisher's Game* (Frank Amato Publications, 2001)

Hanley, Ken. *Fly Fishing the Pacific Inshore* (The Lyons Press, 2003)

Kreh, Lefty. *Fly Fishing in Salt Water* (The Lyons Press, 1997)

Kreh, Lefty. *Presenting the Fly* (The Lyons Press, 1999)

Kreh, Lefty, and Mark Sosin. *Practical Fishing Knots* (The Lyons Press, 1991)